1 MONTH OF
FREE
READING

at
www.ForgottenBooks.com

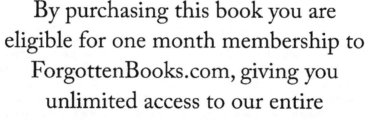

By purchasing this book you are eligible for one month membership to ForgottenBooks.com, giving you unlimited access to our entire collection of over 1,000,000 titles via our web site and mobile apps.

To claim your free month visit:
www.forgottenbooks.com/free232563

ISBN 978-0-483-57060-3
PIBN 10232563

This book is a reproduction of an important historical work. Forgotten Books uses state-of-the-art technology to digitally reconstruct the work, preserving the original format whilst repairing imperfections present in the aged copy. In rare cases, an imperfection in the original, such as a blemish or missing page, may be replicated in our edition. We do, however, repair the vast majority of imperfections successfully; any imperfections that remain are intentionally left to preserve the state of such historical works.

THE FESTIVALS OF OUR LADY.

(From THE GOLDEN LEGEND.)

BY

JACOBUS DE VORAGINE

(Archbishop of Genoa).

LONDON :

TALBOT & CO.,

13, Paternoster Row, E.C.

CONTENTS.

THE VISITATION, *July 2*, is not included in The Golden Legend.

LIST OF ILLUSTRATIONS.

The Nativity of our Blessed Lady.

SEPTEMBER 8.

The nativity of the blessed and glorious Virgin Mary, of the lineage of Judah and of the royal kindred of David took her original beginning. Matthew and Luke describe not the generation of Mary but of Joseph, which was far from the conception of Christ. But the custom of writing was of such ordinance that the generation of women is not showed, but of the men. And verily the blessed Virgin descended of the lineage of David, and it is certain that Jesu Christ was born of this only Virgin. It is certain that He came of the lineage of David and of Nathan, for David had two sons, Nathan and Solomon among all his other sons.

And as John Damascene witnesseth that of Nathan descended Levy, and Levy engendered Melchion and Panthar, Panthar

B

engendered Barpanthar, Barpanthar engendered Joachim, Joachim engendered
the Virgin Mary, which was of the lineage
of Solomon. For Nathan had a wife, of
whom he engendered Jacob, and when
Nathan was dead Melchion, which was
son of Levy and brother of Panthar,
wedded the wife of Nathan, mother of
Jacob, and on her he engendered Eli,
and so Jacob and Eli were brethren of
one mother but not of one father. For
Jacob was of the line of Solomon and Eli
of the line of Nathan, and then Eli of the
line of Nathan died without children, and
Jacob his brother, which was of the line
of Solomon, took a wife and engendered
and raised the seed of his brother and
engendered Joseph.

Joseph then by nature is son of Jacob
by descent of Solomon. That is to wit,
Joseph is the son of Jacob, and after the
law he is son of Eli which descended of
Nathan, for the son that was born, was by
nature his that engendered him, and by
the law he was son of him that was dead,
like as it is said in the Scholastic History.

And Bede witnesseth in his chronicle
that, when all the generations of the
Hebrews and other strangers were kept

in the most secret chests of the temple, Herod commanded them to be burnt, weening thereby to make himself noble among the others. If the proofs of the lineages were failed, he should make them believe that his lineage appertained to them of Israel.

And there were some that were called *dominics*, for because they were so nigh to Jesu Christ and were of Nazareth, and they had learned the order of generation of our Lord, a part of their grandsires' fathers, and a part by some books that they had in their houses and taught them forth as much as they might.

Joachim spoused Anne, which had a sister named Hismeria, and Hismeria had two daughters, named Elizabeth, and Eliud. Elizabeth was mother to John Baptist, and Eliud engendered Eminen. And of Eminen came St. Servatius, whose body lieth in Maestricht, upon the river of the Meuse, in the bishopric of Liège. And Anne had three husbands, Joachim, Cleophas, and Salome; and of the first she had a daughter named Mary, the Mother of God, the which was given to Joseph in marriage, and she childed our Lord Jesu Christ. And when Joachim

was dead, she took Cleophas, the brother
of Joseph, and had by him another daughter named Mary also, and she was married
to Alpheus.   And Alpheus her husband
had by her four sons, that was James the
Less, Joseph the Just, otherwise named
Barsabee, Simon, and Jude.   Then the
second husband being dead, Anne married the third named Salome, and had
by him another daughter which yet also
was called Mary, and she was married to
Zebedee.   And this Mary had of Zebedee
two sons, that is to wit, James the More,
and John the Evangelist.   And hereof be
made these verses :—

Anna solet dici tres concepisse Marias,
Quas genuere viri Joachim, Cleophas Salomeque.
Has duxere viri Joseph, Alpheus, Zebedeus.
Prima parit Christum, Jacobum secunda minorem,
Et Joseph justum peperit cum Simone Judam,
Tertia majorem Jacobum volucremque Johannem.

But it is marvellous for to see how the
blessed Virgin Mary might be cousin of
Elizabeth as it is before said.   It is certain
that Elizabeth was Zachary's wife, which
was of the lineage of Levi, and after the
law each ought to wed a wife of his own
lineage.   And she was of the daughters of
Aaron, as St. Luke witnesseth, and Anne

was of Bethlehem, as St. Jerome saith,
and was of the tribe of Judah.   And then
they of the line of Levi wedded wives of
the line of Judah, so that the line royal
and the line of the priests were always
joined together by cousinage.   So that
as Bede saith :—'This cousinage might
be made sith the first time, and thus to
be nourished from lineage to lineage, and
thus should it be certain that the blessed
Virgin Mary descended of the royal line,
and had cousinage of the priests.'   And
our blessed Lady was of both lineages,
and so our Lord would that these two
lineages should intermingle together for
great mystery.   For it appertaineth that
he should be born and offered for us,
very God, and very king, and very priest,
and should govern his true Christian men
fighting in the chivalry of this life, and to
crown them after their victory, the which
thing appeareth of the name of Christ, for
Christ is as much to say as anointed.   For
in the old law there was none anointed
but priests and kings, and we be called
Christian men of Christ, and be called
the lineage chosen of kings and priests.
But because it is said that the men
took wives of their lineage only, that was

because the distribution of the sorts
should not be confounded. For the
tribe of Levy had not his sort with the
other, and therefore might they well
marry them with the women of that tribe
or where they would, like as St. Jerome
rehearseth in his prologue. When he was
a child he had a little book of the history
of the nativity of the Virgin Mary, but as
he remembered a long time after, he translated it by the prayer of some persons, and
found that Joachim, which was of Galilee
of the city of Nazareth, espoused St. Anne
of Bethlehem, and they were both just and
without reproach or reprehension in the
commandments of our Lord, and divided
all their substance in three parts: that one
part was for the temple, that other they
gave to the poor and pilgrims, and the,
third was for themselves and their household to live with, and thus lived twenty.
years in marriage without having any
lineage.

And then they avowed to our Lord that
if He sent to them any lineage they should
give it to Him, for to serve Him.

For which thing they went every year
into Jerusalem in three principal feasts,
so that in the feast of Encenia, that was

the dedication of the temple, then Joachim went unto Jerusalem with his kindred, and came to the altar with the others and would have offered his offering. And when the priest saw him, he put him apart by great despite, and reproved him because he came to the altar of God, and said to him that it was convenable that a man cursed in the faith should not offer to our Lord, nor he that was barren should be among them that had fruit, as he that had none to the increase of the people of God.

And then Joachim, all confused for this thing, durst not go home for shame, because they of his lineage and his neighbours which had heard it should not reprove him.

And then he went to his herdmen, and was there long, and then the angel appeared to him only, and comforted him with great clearness, and said to him that he should not doubt nor be afraid of his vision, and said :—'I am the angel of our Lord sent to thee for to announce to thee that thy prayers have availed thee and been heard, and thy alms be mounted before our Lord. I have seen thy shame and heard the reproach. That thou art

barren is to thee no reproach by right,
and God is the avenger of sin and not of
nature.   And when He closeth the belly
or womb, He worketh so that He openeth
it after, more marvellously.   And the fruit
that shall be born shall not be seen to
come forth by lechery, but that it be
known that it is of the gift of God.   The
first mother of your people was Sara, and
she was barren unto the ninetieth year,
and had only Isaac, to whom the benediction of all people was promised.   And
was not Rachel long barren?   And yet
had she not after Joseph, that held
all the seigniory of Egypt? which was
more strong than Samson, and more
holy than Samuel?   And yet were their
mothers barren.   Thus mayst thou believe by reason and ; by ensample that
the childings long abiden be wont to
be more marvellous.   And therefore
Anne thy wife shall have a daughter,
and thou shalt call her Mary, and she,
as ye have avowed, shall be from her infancy sacred unto our Lord, and shall be
full of the Holy Ghost sith the time that
she shall depart from the womb of her
mother, and she shall dwell in the temple
of our Lord, and not without, among the

other people, because that none evil thing shall be had in suspicion of her, and right as she shall be born of a barren mother, so shall be born of her marvellously the son of a right high Lord. Of whom the name shall be Jesus, and by Him shall health be given to all the people. And I give to thee the sign, that when thou shalt come to the Golden Gate at Jerusalem, thou shalt meet there Anne thy wife, which is much amoved of thy long tarrying, and shall have joy of thy coming.' And then the angel, when he had said this, he departed from him.

And as when Anne wept bitterly and wist not whither her husband was gone, the same angel appeared to her, and said all that he had said to her husband, and gave to her for a sign that she should go into Jerusalem, to the Golden Gate, and there she should meet with her husband which was returned. And thus by the commandment of the angel they met, and were firm of the lineage promised, and glad for to see each other, and honoured our Lord and returned home, abiding joyously the promise divine. And Anne conceived and brought forth a daughter, and named her Mary.

And then when she had accomplished the time of three years, and had left sucking, they brought her to the temple with offerings.   And there was about the temple, after the fifteen psalms of degrees, fifteen steps or grees to ascend up to the temple, because the temple was high set. And nobody might go to the Altar of Sacrifices that was without, but by the degrees.   And then our Lady was set on the lowest step, and mounted up without any help as she had been of perfect age, and when they had performed their offering, they left their daughter in the temple with the other virgins, and they returned into their place.   And the Virgin Mary profited every day in all holiness, and was visited daily of angels, and had every day divine visions.

Jerome saith in an epistle to Chromatius and to Heliodorus that the blessed Virgin Mary had ordained this custom to herself that, from the morning unto the hour of tierce, she was in orison and prayer, and from tierce unto nones she entended to her work, and from nones she ceased not to pray, till that the angel came and gave to her meat.

And in the fourteenth year of her age,

the bishop commanded in common that the virgins that were instituted in the temple, and had accomplished the time of age, should return to their houses and should after the law be married.

All the others obeyed his commandment, but Mary answered that she might not do so because her father and mother had given her all to the service of our Lord.

And then the bishop was much angry because he durst not make her to break her avow against the scripture, that saith: Avow ye vows and yield them to God. And he durst not break the custom of the people.

And then came a feast of the Jews, and he called all the ancient Jews to council, and showed to them this thing. And this was all their sentence: That in a thing so doubtable, that counsel shall be asked of our Lord. And then went they all to prayer, and the bishop, that was gone to ask counsel of our Lord.

Anon came a voice out of the oracle and said that, all they that were of the house of David that were convenable to be married and had no wife, that each of them should bring a rod to the altar, and

his rod that flourished, and, after the saying of Isaiah, the Holy Ghost sit in the
form of a dove on it, he should be the
man that should be chosen and married
to the Virgin Mary.

And Joseph, of the House of David,
was there among the others, and for him
it seemed to be an inconceivable thing, a
man of so old age as he to have so tender
a maid, and whereas others brought forth
their rods he hid his. And when nothing
appeared according to the voice of God,
the bishop ordained for to ask counsel
again of our Lord. And He answered
that, he only that should espouse the
virgin had not brought forth his rod.
And then Joseph by the commandment
of the bishop brought forth his rod, and
anon it flowered, and a dove descended
from Heaven thereupon, so that it was
clearly the advice of every man that he
should have the virgin.

And then he espoused the Virgin Mary,
and returned into his city of Bethlehem
for to ordain his family and his house,
and to fetch such things as were
necessary.

And the Virgin Mary returned unto
the house of her father with seven virgins,

her fellows of her age, which had seen the demonstrance of the miracle.

And in those days the angel of our Lord appeared to the Virgin praying, and showed to her how the Son of God should be born of her.

And the day of the nativity was not known in long time of good Christian men, and as master John Beleth saith that, it happed that a man of good contemplation every year in the sixth ides of September was in prayer, and he heard a company of angels that made great solemnity. And then he required devoutly that he might have knowledge wherefore every year only on that day he heard such solemnity and not on other days. And then he had a divine answer that, on that day the blessed Virgin Mary was born into this world, and that he should make it to be known to the men of Holy Church, so that they should be concordable to the Heavenly court in hallowing this solemnity.

And when he had told this to the sovereign bishop the pope, and to the others, and had been in fastings, in prayers, and sought in scriptures and witnesses of old writings, they established this day of the Nativity of the glorious Virgin to be hallowed generally of all Christian men ; but the octave was not hallowed nor kept for some time. But Innocent the fourth, of the nation of Genoa, ordained and instituted the said octave to be observed. And the cause was this :—

After the death of Pope Gregory, the citizens of Rome enclosed all the cardinals in the conclave because they should seriously consider the good of the Church ; but they did not agree for many days, and suffered much sorrow from the Romans.

Then avowed they to the Queen of Heaven that if they might go quiet from thence they should establish the observance of the octaves of the nativity which they had long neglected. And they then by one accord chose Celestin as Pope, and were delivered from the conclave, their vow was accomplished by Innocent, for Celestin lived but a little time, and therefore it might not be accomplished by him. And it is to wit that the church halloweth three nativities, the Nativity of our Lord, the Nativity of the blessed Virgin Mary, and the Nativity of St. John

Baptist. And these three signify three nativities spiritual, for we be born again · with St. John Baptist in the water of baptism, and with Mary in penance, and with our Lord Jesu Christ in glory. And it behoveth that nativity of baptism go before contrition, and that of joy also. For the two by reason have vigils, but because that penance is accounted for vigil, therefore that of our Lady behoveth no vigil, but they all have octaves, for all haste them unto the eighth resurrection.

There was a knight very noble and devout unto our Lady, which went to a tourneying, and he found a monastery in his way which was of the Virgin Mary, and entered into it for to hear Mass, and there were Masses one after another, and for the honour of our Lady he would leave none but that he heard them all. And when he issued out of the monastery he hasted him appertly. And they that returned from the tourney met him, and said to him that he had ridden right nobly. And they that hated him affirmed the same, and all they together cried that he had right nobly tourneyed, and some went to him and said that he had taken them. Then he, that was wise, advised him that the courteous Virgin and Queen had so courteously honoured him, and recounted all that was happened, and then returned he to the monastery, and ever after abode in the service of our Lord, the son of the blessed Virgin.

There was a bishop which had the blessed Virgin Mary in sovereign honour and devotion, and there he saw the virgin of all virgins, which came to meet him, and began to lead him by sovereign honour to the church that he went to, and two maidens of the company went before singing and saying these verses:—

Cantemus domino, sociæ, cantemus honorem,
Dulcis amor Christi resonet ore pio.

That is to say: 'Sing we fellows to our Lord, sing we honour. Sing we with a gentle voice that sweet love which ought to please him.' And that other company of virgins sang and rehearsed again the same. Then the first two singers began to sing this that followeth :—

Primus ad ima ruit magna de luce superbus,
Sic homo cum tumuit, primus ad ima ruit.

That is to say: 'The first pride fell low from great light. So the first man, for his eating of the apple, fell low also.' And so they brought the said bishop to the church with procession, and the two in front always began, and the others followed.

There was a widow whose husband was dead, and had a son whom she loved tenderly, and that son was taken with enemies and put in prison fast bound. And when she heard thereof, she wept without comfort, and prayed unto our blessed Lady with right devout prayers that she would deliver her son, and at the last she saw that her prayers availed her not, and entered then into the church wherein the image of our Lady was carved, and stood before the image and reasoned with it in this manner, saying:—'O blessed Virgin, I have prayed oft to thee for my son that thou shouldst deliver him, and thou hast not helped me his wretched mother, and I pray also thy son to help me and yet I feel no fruit. And therefore like as my son is taken from me so shall I take away thine, and set him in prison in hostage for mine.' And in this saying she approached near and took away from the image the child that she held in her lap, and wrapped it in clean clothes and shut it in her chest, and

c

locked it fast right diligently, and was
right joyful that she had so good hostage
for her son, and kept it much diligently.
And the night following, the blessed
Virgin Mary came to the son of the same
widow, and opened to him the door of
the prison, and commanded him to go
thence, and said to him :—'Son, say to
thy mother that she yield to me again
my son since I have delivered her son.'
And he issued and came to his mother,
and told to her how our blessed Lady
had delivered him, and she was joyful,
and took the child and came to the
church and delivered him to our Lady,
saying :—'Lady I thank you, for ye have
delivered to me my son, and here I
deliver to you yours again, for I confess
that I have mine.'

There was a thief that often stole, but
he had always great devotion to the
Virgin Mary, and saluted her oft. It was
so that on a time he was taken and judged
to be hanged. And when he was hanged
the blessed Virgin sustained and hanged
him up with her hands three days that
he died not nor had any hurt, and they
that hanged him passed by, and found
him living and of glad cheer. And then

they supposed that the cord had not been well strained, and would have slain him with a sword, and have cut his throat, but our blessed Lady set on her hand before the strokes so that they might not slay him nor grieve him, and then they knew by that he told to them that the blessed Mother of God helped him, and then they marvelled, and took him off and let him go in the honour of the Virgin Mary, and then he went and entered into a monastery, and was in the service of the Mother of God as long as he lived.

There was a clerk that loved much the blessed Virgin, and said his hours every day ententively. And when his father and mother were dead, they had none other heir so that he had all the heritage, and then he was constrained of his friends that he should take a wife and govern his own heritage. And on a day it happed that they intended to hold the feast of his marriage, and as he was going to the wedding he came to a church, and he remembered of the service of our blessed Lady, and entered in and began to say his hours. And the blessed Virgin Mary appeared to him and spake to him a little cruelly :— 'O fool and unhappy, why hast thou left

me that am thy spouse and thy friend, and
lovest another woman before me?' Then
he, being moved, returned to his fellows
and feigned all, and left to accomplish the
sacrament of marriage. And when mid-
night came he left all and fled out of the
house, and entered into a monastery and
there served the Mother of God.

There was a priest of a parish, which
was of honest and good life, and could say
no Mass but Mass of our Lady, the which
he sang devoutly in the honour of her,
wherefore he was accused before the
bishop, and was anon called before him.
And the priest confessed that he could say
none other Mass, wherefore the bishop
reproved him sore as incapable and an
idiot, and suspended him of his Mass,
that he should no more sing any from
that time. And then our blessed Lady
appeared to the bishop and blamed him
much because he had so treated her
chaplain, and said to him that he should
die within thirty days if he failed to re-
establish him again to his accustomed
office. Then the bishop was afeard, and
sent for the priest and prayed him of for-
giveness, and bade him that he should
not sing but of our Lady.

There was a clerk which was vain and
riotous, but always he loved much our
Lady, the Mother of God, and said every
day his hours. And he saw on a night a
vision that, he was in judgment before our
Lord, and our Lord said to them that
were there:—'What judgment shall we do
of this clerk? devise ye it for I have long
suffered him, and see no sign yet of
amendment.' Then our Lord gave upon him sentence of damnation, and all
they approved it. Then arose the blessed
Virgin and said to her son:—'I pray thee,
gentle son, of thy mercy for this man, so
that thou assuage upon him the sentence
of damnation, and that, by the grace of me,
he which is condemned to death by his
merits may live yet.' And our Lord said
to her:—'I deliver him at thy request, for
to know if I shall see his correction.'
Then our Lady turned her toward him
and said:—'Go, and sin no more lest it
happen worse to thee.' Then he awoke,
and changed his life, and entered into
religion, and finished his life in good
works.

. In the year of our Lord five hundred.
and thirty-seven, there was a man named
Theophilus which was vicar of a bishop,

as Fulbert saith, that was bishop of Chartres. And this Theophilus wisely dispensed the goods of the church under the bishop; and when the bishop was dead, all the people said that this vicar should be bishop. But he said the office of vicar sufficed him, and had sooner that than to be made bishop, so there was there another bishop made, and Theophilus was, against his will, put out of his office.

Then he fell in despair, in such wise that he counselled with a Jew how he should have his office again. Now this Jew was a magician, and called the devil, and he came anon. Then Theophilus, by the commandment of the devil, denied God and His Mother, and renounced his Christian profession, and wrote an obligation with his blood and sealed it with his ring, and delivered it to the devil, and thus he was brought into his office again.

And on the morn Theophilus was received into the grace of the bishop by the procuration of the devil, and was re-established in the dignity of his office. And afterwards, when he advised himself, he repented and sorrowed sore of this

that he had done, and ran with great
devotion unto the Virgin Mary, with all
devotion of his thought, praying her to be
his aid and help. And then on a time our
blessed Lady appeared to him in vision,
and rebuked him of his felony, and commanded him to forsake the devil, and
made him to confess Jesu Christ to be
son of God, and to knowledge himself to
be in purpose to be a Christian man, and
thus he recovered the grace of her and of
her son. And in sign of pardon that she
had gotten him, she delivered to him
again his obligation that he had given to
the devil, and laid it upon his breast so
that he should never doubt to be servant
of the devil, but he enjoyed that he was
so delivered by our blessed Lady.

When Theophilus had heard all this he
was very joyful, and told it to the bishop
and before all the people what was befallen him, and all marvelled greatly, and
gave laud and praising unto the glorious
Virgin, our Lady, St. Mary. And three
days after he rested in peace.

There be many other miracles which
our blessed Lady hath showed for them
that call upon her, which were over long
to write here, but as touching her nativity

this sufficeth. Then let us continually give laud and praising to her as much as we may, and let us say with St. Jerome this response : *Sancta et immaculata virginitas.* And how this holy response was made, I purpose, under correction, to write here.

It is so that I was at Cologne, and heard rehearsed there by a noble doctor that the holy and devout St. Jerome had a custom to visit the churches at Rome. And so he came into a church where an image of our blessed Lady stood in a chapel by the door as he entered, and passed forthby without any salutation to our Lady, and went forth to every altar and made his prayers to all the saints in the church, each after other, and returned again by the same image without any saluting to her. Then our blessed Lady called him and spake to him by the said image, and demanded of him the cause why he made no salutation to her, seeing that he had done honour and worship to all the other saints of whom the images were in that church. And then St. Jerome knelt down and said thus : *Sancta et immaculata virginitas, quibus te laudibus referam nescio. Quia quem celi capere non poterant, tuo gremio contulisti.* Which is to say : Holy and undefiled virginity, I wot never what laud and praisings I shall give to thee. For him that all the heavens might not take nor contain, thou hast born in thy womb.

So since this holy man thought himself insufficient to give to her laud, then what shall we sinful wretches do but put us wholly in her mercy, acknowledging us insufficient to give to her due laud and praising ? But let us meekly beseech her to accept our good intent and will, and that by her merits we may attain after this life to come to her in ever-lasting life in Heaven. Amen.

The Immaculate Conception.

Murillo.

To face 27.

The Conception of our Lady.

DECEMBER 8.

Maria invenisti graciam apud Dominum.
Lucæ primo capitulo.

When the angel Gabriel had greeted our Lady, to show to her the conception of our Lord, and to take from her all doubts and dreads, he comforted her in saying the words aforesaid : Mary, thou hast found grace at the Lord.

There be four manners of people, of which the two be good and the two be evil. For some there be that seek not God nor His grace, as people out of the belief, of whom may be said as it is written :—'Who that believeth not on his Lord God shall die perpetually.' And other there be that seek God and His grace, but they find it not, for they seek it not as they ought to do, but as covetous men that set all their love in riches and in solace of the world.

Such people be likened to them that seek flowers in winter: well seek they flowers in winter that seek God and His grace in the covetousness of the world, which is so cold of all virtues that it quencheth all the devotion of the love of God.

And well is called the world winter in Holy Scripture; for its evils and vices make men sinners and cold to serve God. And therefore saith the Holy Ghost to the soul that is amorous, *Canticorum, cap. ii:* 'Arise up thou my fair soul, the winter is past.' *Jam enim hiems transiit.* For thou hast vanquished the temptations of the world which kill My love, and therefore come into My realm where thou shalt find delight in all flowers of the summer, whereas the sinners may not come, because they seek not God as they ought to do by very repentance of heart.

And therefore saith our Lord, *Johannis, cap. vii, Quæretis me et non invenietis. Item Johannis, cap. viii, Et quæretis me et in peccato vestro moriemini.* 'Ye seek Me and find Me not.' Item: 'So ye seek Me and in sin shall ye die.'

The third manner of people that seek not God, and yet nevertheless they find

Him; they be children that die in their innocency and be purged by baptism. Of whom God said by his prophet Isaiah, cap. lxv, *Invenerunt qui non quæsierunt me.* 'I am found of them that sought Me not'; and that is for default of age.

The fourth manner of people that seek God and find Him, be they that set all their desire to serve God and love Him, like as the blessed Virgin Mary, that since she was in her infancy, she ever put her in the service of God and love of Him, and vowed to Him chastity, before all other women.

Therefore with right, might the angel well say to her: *Maria, invenisti graciam apud dominum:* 'Mary, thou hast found grace at God our Lord.'

We find in the scripture that this glorious Virgin Mary hath found grace in three manners; for her coming was long before prophesied, and her birth announced and showed by the angel; and in the womb of her mother ere she was born, sanctified and hallowed.

First her coming was showed and prophesied in many manners, and by many figures, for Balaam prophesied, *Numeri, cap. xxiv, Orietur stella ex Jacob, et*

consurget virga de Israel.   That is to say,
that the Virgin Mary shall be born of the
lineage of Jacob patriarch.   It is a custom that when folk will praise a person,
they will compare him to a valiant man,
like as it is said commonly of a hardy
man :—'This is a right Alexander'; and
of a simple man :—'This is a right Job.'
Thus Balaam the prophet compared our
Lady to a star for three causes.   First, for
that she is adorned and giveth beauty to
all human creatures like as the star doth
on the firmament, for she hath opened
to us the gate of Paradise; like as it is
sung in Holy Church : *Paradisi porta per
Evam cunctis clausa est, et per beatam
Virginem Mariam iterum patefacta est:*
'The gate of paradise, which by Eve was
closed from all men, is now opened by
the blessed Virgin Mary.'

Secondly, like as the star enlumineth
the night by his clearness, in like wise the
glorious lady enlumineth by her life all
Holy Church.   Whereof Holy Church
singeth : *Cujus vita gloriosa lucem dedit
seculo:* 'The noble life of our Lady giveth
light to all churches.'   For as saith Hugo
de Sancto Victore:—'O glorious Lady, forasmuch as thou hast engendered a grace

and glory to all manner of people, unto
the dead life, to sinners grace, and to
caitiffs pardon,' may be said as is said,
*Judith, cap. xv, Tu gloria Jerusalem, tu
lætitia Israel, tu honorificentia, etc.*: 'Thou
art the glory of Jerusalem, thou art the
joy of Israel, thou art all the honour of
our people.' *Cap. eodem : Confortatum
est cor tuum, eo quod castitatem amaveris,
et post virum tuum, alterum nescieris: ideo
et manus Domini confortavit te, et ideo eris
benedicta in æternum :*—'Thou hast kept
chastity, and therefore thou shalt be eternally blessed.' *Judith viii, Ora pro nobis,
quoniam mulier sancta es, etc. Item,
cap. xiv, Benedicta es, etc.* It was said
to Judith the widow, this that we may
say to our Lady :—'Pray for us for ye be
an holy woman, ye be a daughter that is
blessed of the sovereign God above all
the women that be on the earth.'

Thirdly, she is compared to the star, for
she hath dwelled all her life stedfastly in
all works of virtue, without doing any sin,
like as the star holdeth him on the firmament without descending to the earth.
For as St. Bernard saith :—'If it were
demanded to all the saints that ever have
been: have ye been without sin?' Except

the glorious Virgin Mary, they might answer this that is written, *Johannis, cap. i, Si dixerimus quoniam non peccavimus, etc.* :—'If we say that we have done no sin, we deceive ourselves, and the truth is not in us.'

This glorious virgin was, in the womb of her mother, sanctified more plainly and more specially than ever was any other, for as saith St. Thomas Aquinas in Compendio :—'There be three manners of sanctifications, the first is common, and given by the sacraments of the Holy Church, like as by baptism and other sacraments, and these give grace but to take away the inclination to sin deadly and venially, nay, and this was done in the Virgin Mary, for she was hallowed and confirmed in all goodness, more than ever was any creature, like as saith St. Austin :—'She did never sin mortal nor venial.' For she was so much enlumined by the Holy Ghost which descended in her, that through the conception of her blessed son Jesu Christ, which rested in her nine months, she was so confirmed in all virtues that there abode in her no inclination of sin. And therefore the Holy Church doth her more reverence and honour in ordaining to hallow the feast of her conception, because this feast is common to the knowledge of Holy Church by some miracles, like as we find reading in this manner :—

'Anselm, Archbishop of Canterbury and pastor of England, sendeth greeting and benediction in our Lord perpetual unto the bishops that be under me, and to all them that have remembrance of the blessed Virgin Mary mother of God.

'Right dear brethren, how the conception of the glorious Virgin Mary hath been showed sometime in England, in France, and in other countries by miracles, I shall rehearse to you.

'In the time that it pleased to God for to correct the people of England of their evils and sins, and to constrain them to His service, He gave victory in battle to William, the glorious Duke of Normandy, to win and conquer the realm of England. And soon after that he was king of the land, he, by the help of God, and of his prudence, reformed the estates and dignities of Holy Church into better reformation than it had been, to which the devil, enemy unto all good works had envy; and it pained him to hinder and let the

D

good works, as well by falseness of his servants as by encumbering of his strangers.

'For when the Danes heard say that England was subject unto the Normans, immediately they made them ready to withstand it.

'When king William understood this, he sent the Abbot of Rumsey, which was named Helsinus, into Denmark for to know the truth.

'This abbot after he had well and diligently done the charge of his commission, and was returned a great part of the sea homeward, there arose a great tempest on the sea, in such wise that the cords and other habiliments of the ship brake. And the masters and governors of the ship, and all they that were therein, lost the hope and trust to escape the peril of this tempest, and all cried devoutly to the glorious Virgin Mary, which is comfort to the discomforted, and hope to the despairing, and recommended themselves in the keeping of God. And thereupon they saw coming towards the ship, upon the water, an honourable person in habit of a bishop, which called the said abbot in the ship, and said to him: "Wilt thou escape these perils of the sea, and go home whole and

safe into thy country?" And the abbot
answered, weeping, that he desired that
above all other things. Then said the
angel to him: "Know thou that I am sent
hither by our Lady to say to thee that if
thou wilt hear me and do thereafter, thou
shalt escape this peril of the sea." The
abbot promised that gladly he would obey
to that he should say. Then said the
angel: "Make covenant to God, and to
me, that thou shalt hallow the feast of the
Conception of our Lady, and of her creation, well and solemnly, and that thou
shalt go and preach it." And the abbot
demanded in what time this feast should be
kept. The angel answered to him, "The
eighth day of December." And the abbot
demanded him what office and service he
should take for the service in Holy Church.
And the angel answered: "All the office
of the Nativity of our Lady, save where
thou sayest *nativity,* thou shalt say, *conception,*" and thereupon, after the angel
vanished away, the tempest ceased.

'And the abbot came home safely into
his country with his company, and noti-
fied to all them that he might, that he
had heard and seen. And, right dear sirs,
if ye will arrive at the port of health, let

us hallow devoutly the creation and the conception of the mother of our Lord, by whom we may receive the reward of her son in the glory of Celestial Paradise.'

It is also otherwise declared:—In the time of Charlemagne, king of France, there was a clerk which was brother germain to the king of Hungary, which loved heartily the blessed Virgin Mary and was wont to say every day matins of her, and the Hours. It happed that by counsel of his friends he took in marriage a very fair damsel, and when he had wedded her, and the priest had given the benediction on them after the Mass, he remembered that that day he had not said his Hours of our Lady, wherefore he sent home the bride, his wife, and the people, to his house, and he abode in the church beside an altar for to say his Hours; and when he came to this anthem: *Pulchra es et decora filia Jerusalem*—that is to say:—'Thou art fair and gracious, daughter of Jerusalem,' there appeared before him the glorious Virgin Mary with two angels on either side, and said to him:—'I am fair and gracious, wherefore leavest thou me and takest thou another wife? or where hast thou seen one more fair than I am?' And the

clerk answered : — ' Madam, thy beauty
surmounteth all the beauty of the world,
thou art lift up above the heavens and
above the angels; what wilt thou that I
do?' And she answered and said :—'If
thou wilt leave thy wife fleshly, thou shalt
have me thy spouse in the realm of
Heaven, and if thou wilt hallow the feast
of my conception, the eighth day of December, and preach it about that it may
be hallowed, thou shalt be crowned in
the realm of Heaven.' And therewith our
Blessed Lady vanished away.

Let us then pray to that glorious virgin
our Lady Saint Mary, that we after this
short and transitory life may be crowned
in Heaven in celestial glory, to which God
bring us. Amen.

The Purification.   *Carpaccio.*

The Purification of our Lady.

Postquam impleti sunt dies purgationis Marie secundum legem Moisi, tulerunt Jesum in Jerusalem. Lucæ, cap. ii.

The ancient law had his course until the time that God hath suffered death for us. And when He died on the cross He said, *Joh., cap. xix., Consummatum est,* that is to say :—'All thing is finished and ended that hath been written of me.' Which law He kept during his life; as it is written :—'I am not come for to break the law'; in which He gave us example of humility and of obedience, like as St. Paul saith.

In like wise our Lady, for to obey to the law, bare her sweet son Jesu Christ unto the temple of Jerusalem after the fortieth day of His birth, for to offer Him to God, and for to give offering for Him such as in the law was ordained, that is to wit, a pair of turtles or two doves was the offering of poor folk, like as it is written.

Our Lord, which in all case came to make our salvation, deigned not only to humble Himself and descend from His realm, and became man mortal, insemblable to us. Also He deigned to be born of a poor woman, and was poor for to enrich us, and draw us out of the misery of this world to eternal riches. And we that be poor because of our sins, and without riches of good virtues, so worthily should we come and be at the feast of our Lord; we should offer to Him that which by the offering is signified.

The dove which is of her nature simple and without gall, and the turtle naturally chaste, for when she hath lost her mate she will never have other mate, and with that she taketh the weeping for her song; we ought to offer to our Lord instead of two doves, one simple will and a good intention, without retaining in our heart any gall of anger or of hate towards our neighbour; for as our Lord saith, if thine eye be simple all thy works shall be in light.

And hereof saith St. John the Evangelist in the Apocalypse :—'The city needeth no sun nor moon to shine in it, for the clearness of God shall illumine it, and his lantern is the Lamb; the Lamb is the Light. By the lamb, which is simple, is signified to us a simple conscience and righteous, which maketh true judgment of the intention, for all works be good or evil.

If they be done in evil intention or by hypocrisy they be evil and without profit, like as saith Jesu Christ:—'If thine eye be evil, all thy body shall be dark.' By the eye is understood the intention, with goodness simple, and gentleness is signified by the doves. We ought also to offer a pair of turtles to our Lord, that is to say, a chaste life and a very intention to leave our sins, the which is signified to us by the chastity of the turtle, and by her weeping the contrition.

As Bede saith :—'Contrition ought to begin in dread and end in love'; for the faithful soul, when she remembereth her sins in her conscience, weepeth for the dread of the pains of hell that she hath deserved, and thus offereth she to God a turtle; and when she hath wept, there cometh to her a hope to have mercy and

pardon of her sins, and this hope is conceived of dread in him and love of God,
to serve and to be in His company; so
that soul that ought to sing, weepeth for
love, which hath delivered her so soon
from the perils and miseries of this world,
and for to come to the sweet company
of our Lord.   And thus offered she that
other turtle, in weeping with David the
prophet the long pilgrimages that she
hath made in the miseries of this world
saying: *Heu me quia incolatus meus
prolongatus est;* for when she beginneth
to think after the joyous company of angels, and of the souls that be in Heaven,
and what joy and delight that they have
in the over-desirous sight of our Lord,
then all the world grieveth them, and they
desire to be delivered from the works of
the body for to go into the company of
these holy souls.

And also that St. Simeon, which by
revelation of the Holy Ghost came into
the temple of Jerusalem in the same hour
that the blessed Virgin brought her dear
son for to offer him, and the Holy Ghost
had showed to him, that before he should
die he should see Jesu Christ come in to
the earth, the which birth he knew long

before to be showed by the prophets. And when he saw Jesu Christ brought into the temple, immediately he knew Him by the Holy Ghost to be very God and very man, and took Him between his arms and said:—'Fair Lord God let Thy sergeant and servant from henceforth be in peace, and suffer that after this revelation showed to me, I may depart and die for to be delivered from the evils of this world, for mine corporal and spiritual eyes have seen Thy blessed son Jesu Christ, which shall save the human creatures from their sins; the which Thou hast made ready and ordained before the face of all human creatures, for to be light to all people by His doctrine, to illumine and take away darknesses,' that is to say, of their idolatry.

After this that Isaiah the prophet hath prophesied of Him:—*Populus gentium qui ambulabat in tenebris, etc.*, the people, gentiles or heathen, which walked in darkness to worship idols and devils for very God, saw a great light when they issued from their sins by the doctrine of Jesu Christ which came also to the glory of the Jews, for they received His sight bodily, like as was promised them by the witness of the

prophets, by which they might glorify
them of this, that their rightful King was
born among them and conversed bodily
in their country.

And St. Simeon said : *Nunc dimittis
servum tuum domine, etc.* 'Sire, let Thy
servant depart in peace after Thy word, for
mine eyes have seen Thy health, which
Thou hast made ready before the face of
all peoples, that is light to the revelation
of heathen and to the glory of Thy people
of Israel.'

Jesu Christ is called peace, health, light
and joy. Peace, because that He is our
mediator and our advocate; health, for He
is our redeemer; light, for He is our in-
former; and glory, for He is our governor.

This feast is called Candlemas, and is
made in remembrance of the offering that
our Lady offered in the temple as is said,
and every one beareth this day a candle
of wax burning, which representeth our
Lord Jesu Christ.

Like as the candle burning hath three
things in it, that is to wit, the wax, the
wick, and the fire, right so be three things
in Jesu Christ, that is the body, the soul
and the godhead. For the wax which is
made of the bee purely, without company

and mixture of one bee with another, signifieth the body of our Lord Jesu Christ, and
the fire of the candle signifieth the divinity
of our Lord Jesu Christ, which illumineth
all creatures.

And therefore if we will appear in this
feast before the face of God, pure and
clean and acceptable, we ought to have
in us three things which be signified by
the candle burning: that is good deeds,
true faith, with good works.

And like as the candle without burning
is dead, right so faith is dead without
works as St. James saith, for to believe
in God without obeying His commandments profiteth nothing. And therefore
saith St. Gregory:—'The good work ought
to show withoutforth that thy intention
abide good withinforth the heart, without
seeking within any vain glory to be allowed
and praised.' And by the fire is understood charity, of which God saith : I am
come to put fire in the earth, and whom I
will, I will burn.

This feast is called the Purification of
our Lady, not for that she had need nor
ought make her purification, for she was
pure and clean without having of any
touch of deadly nor venial sin, like as she

that had, without company of any man,
by the virtue of the Holy Ghost, conceived
the Son of God, and was delivered without the loss of her virginity. So she came
with her blessed son at the fortieth day
after His nativity to obey the commandment of the law after the manner of other
women which had need of purification,
and also to show to us the example of
humility. He is very humble that is
worthy to be praised for his virtues.

This glorious Lady is Queen of Heaven
and Lady of Angels, nevertheless she is
pure and humble among the women like
as a poor woman, without making any
semblance of her great humility, nor of
the high majesty of her son, whereof St.
Bernard saith in this manner :—

'O who may make us to understand,
glorious Lady, the thought of thine heart
that thou haddest among the services that
thou madest to thy blessed son in giving
Him suck, in laying down and raising,
when thou sawest a little child of thee
born on that one part, and of that other
side thou knewest Him to be God Almighty?

'And now thou believest and seest Him
created that had created all the world,
now thou seest Him feeble as a child

which is Almighty and all powerful, now
thou feedest Him that all the world
feedeth, and now thou seest Him not
speaking, that made man and speech.

'O who should be able to show hereupon
the secrets of thine heart? How savoured
thy courage when thou heldest thy child
between thine arms whom thou lovedest
as thy Lord, and kissed Him as thy son.
Who should not marvel of this miracle,
when a virgin and a clean maid hath en-
fanted and childed her maker and Lord
of all the world? To Him let us address
our thoughts, and embrace we this child
of one very belief, whom we ought to love
because He hath humbled himself for us,
and to doubt Him, because He is our
judge and our Lord, to whose commandments we owe to obey if we will be saved.'

We read an example of a noble lady
which had great devotion in the blessed
Virgin Mary, and she had a chapel in
which she did do say Mass of our Lady
daily by her chaplain.

It happed that the day of the Purification of our Lady, her chaplain was out,
so that this lady might that day have no
Mass, and she durst not go to another
church because she had given her mantle

unto a poor man for the love of our Lady. She was very sorrowful because she might hear no Mass and for to make her devotions she went into the chapel, and before the altar she kneeled down for to make her prayers to our Lady.

And after a time she fell asleep, in which she had a vision, and it seemed that she was in a church, and saw come into the church a great company of virgins, before whom she saw come a right noble virgin crowned right preciously.

And when they were all set each in order, there came a company of young men which sat down each after the other in order like the other; after, entered one that bare a burden of candles, and gave them to them, the highest first, and so to each of them by order he gave one, and at the last came this man to this lady aforesaid and gave to her also a candle of wax.

The which lady saw also come a priest, a deacon and a sub-deacon, all revested, going to the altar as for to say Mass. And it seemed to her that St. Laurence and St. Vincent were deacon and sub-deacon, and Jesu Christ the priest; and two angels bearing candles before them.

And two young angels began the introit of the Mass, and all the company of the virgins sang the Mass.

And when the Mass was sung unto the offering, it seemed that the virgin so crowned went before, and after, all the others followed, and kneeling much devoutly, offered their candles to the priest.

And when the priest tarried for this lady that she should also have come to the offering, the glorious queen of virgins sent to her to say that she was not courteous to make the priest so long to tarry for her. And the lady answered that the priest should proceed in his Mass forth, for she would keep her candle and not offer it.

And the glorious virgin sent yet again to her, and she said she would not offer her candle.

The third time the queen said to he messenger:—'Go and pray her that she come and offer her candle, or else take it from her by force.' The messenger came to this lady, and because she would in no wise come and offer up her candle, he set hand on the candle that this lady held and drew fast, and she held fast, and so long he drew and haled that the candle

E

brake in two pieces, and that one half
abode still in the hand of the lady aforesaid, which thereupon awoke and came to
herself, and found the piece of the candle
in her hand, whereof she much marvelled,
and thanked our Lord and the glorious
Virgin Mary devoutly which had suffered
her that day not to be without Mass.

And all the days of her life after she
kept that piece of that candle most preciously, like an holy relic, and all they
that were touched therewith were nourished and healed of their maladies and
sicknesses.

Let us pray then humbly to the glorious
Virgin Mary, which is comfort to them
that forsake their sins, that she will make
our peace to the blessed Son and to beseech and get of Him remission of all our
sins, and after this life to come to the
glory and joy of heaven, to the which
bring us the Father, the Son, and the
Holy Ghost.   Amen.

To face 51.

The
Annunciation or Salutation
of the
Angel Gabriel to our Lady.

---x---

MARCH 25.

The feast of this day is called the Annunciation of our Lady, for on this day the angel Gabriel showed to the glorious Virgin Mary the coming of the Blessed Son of God. That is to wit, how He ought to come into the glorious Virgin, and take on her nature and human flesh for to save the world.

It was a well reasonable thing that the angel should come to the glorious Virgin Mary, for like as Eve by the exhorting of the devil gave her consent to do the sin of inobedience to our perdition, right so by the greeting of the angel Gabriel and by exhorting, the glorious Virgin Mary gave her consenting to his message by obedience, to our salvation.

Wherefore like as the first woman was the cause of our damnation, so was the blessed Virgin Mary the beginning of our redemption.

When that the angel Gabriel was sent for to show the Incarnation of our Saviour Jesu Christ, he found her alone, enclosed in her chamber, like as St. Bernard saith, in which the maidens and virgins ought to abide in their houses, without running abroad out openly, and they ought also to flee the words of men, of which their honour and good renoun might be lessened or hurt.

And the angel said to the glorious Virgin Mary:—'I salute thee, full of grace, the Lord is with thee.' In no other place in Scripture is found such a salutation.

And it was brought from Heaven unto the glorious Virgin Mary, which was the first woman in the world that ever offered to God her virginity.

And the angel said to her after :—' Thou shalt be blessed above all other women, for thou shalt escape the malediction that all other women have in childing in sin and in sorrow ; and thou shalt be mother of God, and shalt abide a pure virgin and clean.'

And our blessed Lady was much abashed of this salutation, and thought in herself the manner thereof. This was a good manner of a virgin that so wisely held her still and spake not, and showing example to virgins, which ought not lightly to speak, nor without advice nor manner to answer.

And when the angel knew that for this salutation she was timorous and abashed, he reassured her, saying:—'Mary, be nothing afeared, for thou hast truly found grace at God, for thou art chosen above all women for to receive His blessed Son and be mother to God, and mediator and advocate for to set peace between God and man, to destroy death and bring life.' 'O thou that art a virgin,' saith St. Ambrose, 'learn of Mary to be mannered and fearful to all men, learn to be still and to eschew all dissolutions.'

Mary was afeared of the salutation of the angel, the which said:—'Thou shalt conceive and bring forth a son, and thou shalt call his name Jesus, and He shall be called the Son of God.' And Mary said to the angel:—'In what manner may this be that thou sayest? For I have purposed in mine heart that I shall never know man, and yet I never knew none, how then shall I have a child against the course of nature, and may abide a virgin?'

Then the angel informed her, and began to say how her virginity should be saved in the conceiving of the Son of God, and answered to her in this manner: The Holy Ghost shall come in to thee, which shall make thee to conceive: the manner how thou shalt conceive thou shalt know better than I shall say, for that shall be the work of the Holy Ghost, which of thy blood and of thy flesh shall form purely in the body of the child that thou shalt bear, and other work to this conception shalt thou not do.   And the sovereign virtue of God shall shadow thee in such wise that thou shalt never feel in thee any burning nor carnal covetousness, and shall purge thine heart from all temporal desires, and yet shall the Holy Ghost shadow thee with the corporal mantle, that the blessed Son of God shall be hid in thee and of thee for to cover the right excellent glory of His divinity; so that by this ombre or shadow may be known and seen His dignity; like as Hugh of St. Victor and St. Bernard say.

After, the angel said :—'And for as much as thou shalt conceive of the Holy Ghost and not of man, the child that shall be born of thee shall be called the Son of God.' Vet of this conception which is above nature, the angel said to her this example :—' Lo ! Elizabeth thy cousin, which is barren, hath conceived a child in her age, for there is nothing impossible to God, which is almighty.' Then said the glorious Virgin Mary to the angel the answer for which he was come :—'Lo ! the handmaid of God, He do to me that He hath ordained after thy words.' She hath given to us example to be humble when prosperity of high riches cometh to us, for the first word that she spake or said when she was made mother of God and Queen of Heaven, that was that she called herself ancille or hand-maid, and not lady. Much people is humble in low estate and but few in high estate, that is to wit in great estates, and therefore is humility more praised in them that be great in estate. As soon as she said :—'Lo ! here the handmaid of God, let it be done to me after thy words.'

Thomas says in that same time that she had thus given her assent to the angel, she conceived in her Jesu Christ, which in that same hour was in her, perfect Man and perfect God in one Person; and as wise as He was in heaven, or when He was thirty years old.

This blessed Annunciation happened the twenty-fifth day of the month of March, on which day happened also, as well before as after, these things that hereafter be named.

On that same day Adam, the first man, was created and fell into original sin by inobedience, and was put out of terrestrial paradise.

Also that same day of the month Cain slew Abel his brother. Also Melchisedech made offering to God of bread and wine in the presence of Abraham. Also on the same day Abraham offered Isaac his son.

That same day St. John Baptist was beheaded, and St. Peter was that day delivered out of prison, and St. James the Great, that day was beheaded of Herod. And our Lord Jesu Christ was on that day crucified, wherefore that is a day of great reverence.

Of the salutation that the angel brought to the glorious Virgin, we read an example of a noble knight which for to amend his life gave and rendered himself into an abbey of Citeaux, and, forasmuch as he was no clerk, there was assigned to him a master for to teach him, and to be with the brethren clerks, but he could learn nothing for a long time that he was there save these two words : *Ave Maria,* which words he had so sore imprinted in his heart that alway he had them in his mouth wheresomever he was. At last he died and was buried in the church-yard of the brethren.

It happed after, that upon the grave grew a right fair fleur-de-lis, and in every flower was written in letters of gold : *Ave Maria,* of which miracle all the brethren were amarvelled, and they did open the sepulchre, and found that the root of this fleur-de-lis came out of the mouth of the said knight, and thereupon they understood that our Lord would have him honoured for the great devotion that he had to say these words : *Ave Maria.*

Another knight there was that had a fair place beside the highway where much people passed, whom he robbed as much as he might, and so he used his life. But he had a good custom, for every day he

saluted the glorious Virgin Mary, in saying, *Ave Maria ;* and for no labour he left
not to greet our Lady, as is said.

It happed that an holy man passed by
his house, whom he robbed and de-
spoiled, but that holy man prayed them
that robbed him that they would bring
him to their master for he had to speak
with him in his house of a secret thing
for his profit.

And when the robbers heard that they
led him before the knight their lord ; and
thereupon the holy man prayed him that
he would summon all his household before
him.   And when, by the commandment
of the knight, his men were assembled,
the holy man said :—'Yet be they not
all here ; there is one yet to come.' Then
one of them perceived that the chamberlain of the lord was not come ; and
the knight made him to come immediately.   And when the holy man saw
him come, thereupon he said :—'I con
jure thee by the virtue of Jesu Christ
our Lord that thou say to us who thou
art, and for what cause thou art come
hither.' Thereupon the chamberlain answered :—'Alas, now must I say and
knowledge myself, I am no man but am

a devil which am in the form of a man and have taken it fourteen years, by which space I have dwelled with this knight, for my master hath sent me hither to the end that I should take heed night and day that if this knight ceased to say the salutation, *Ave Maria*, for then I should strangle him with mine own hand and bring him to hell because of the evil life that he hath led and leadeth. But because he saith every day this salutation, *Ave Maria*, I might not have him, and therefore I abode here so long, for there passeth him no day but that he saluteth our Lady.'

When the knight heard this he was much afeard, and fell down to the feet of this holy man and demanded pardon of his sins.

After this the holy man said to the devil:—'I command thee in the name of our Lord that thou depart hence, and go into another place where thou mayst grieve nor annoy no man.'

Then let us pray to the glorious Virgin Mary that she keep us from the devil, and that we may by her come to the glory of Heaven, to the which bring us the Father, the Son, and the Holy Ghost. Amen.

The Assumption.
Raphael.

To face 61.

The Assumption of the Glorious Virgin our Lady St. Mary.

We find in a book sent to St. John the Evangelist, or else the book, which is said to be apocryphal, is ascribed to him, in what manner the Assumption of the blessed Virgin Mary was made. The Apostles were departed and gone in to divers countries of the world for cause of preaching, and the blessed Lady and Virgin was in a house by the Mount of Sion, and as long as she lived she visited all the places of her son with great devotion, that is to say, the place of His baptism, of His fasting, of His passion, of His sepulture, of His Resurrection, and of His Ascension.

And after that Epiphanius saith, she lived four-and-twenty years after the Ascension of her son, and he saith also :—

'When our Lady had conceived Jesu
Christ she was of the age of fourteen
years, and she was delivered in her fif-
teenth year, and lived and abode with
Him three-and-thirty years.' And after
His death she lived four-and-twenty years,
and by this account when she departed
out of this world she was seventy-two
years old; but it is more probable that
which is read in another place, that she
lived after the Ascension of her son
twelve years, and so then she was sixty
years old.

And on a day, when all the Apostles
were spread through the world in preaching, the glorious Virgin was greatly smitten
with the desire to be with her son Jesu
Christ, and her courage was chaffed and
moved, and great abundance of tears ran
withoutforth, because she had not equally
the comforts of her son, which were with-
drawn from her for the time.

And an angel came before her, with
great light, and saluted her honourably
as the mother of his Lord, saying :—'All
hail ! blessed Mary, receiving the blessing
of Him that sent His blessing to Jacob, lo!
here a bough of palm of paradise, Lady,
which I have brought to thee, which thou

shalt command to be borne before thy bier. For thy soul shall be taken from thy body the third day next following, and thy son abideth thee, His honourable mother.' To whom she answered :—'If I have found grace before thine eyes, I pray thee that thou vouchsafe to show to me thy name, and yet I pray thee more heartily that my sons and my brethren the Apostles may be assembled with me, so that before I die I may see them with my bodily eyes, and after, to be buried of them, and they being here, I may yield up my ghost to God. And also yet I pray and require that my spirit, issuing out of the body, see not the horrible nor wicked spirit nor fiend, and that no might of the devil come against me.' And then the angel said :—'Lady, wherefore desirest thou to know my name? which is great and marvellous. All the Apostles shall assemble this day to thee and shall make to thee noble exequies at thy passing, and in the presence of them thou shalt give up thy spirit. For He that brought the prophet by his hair from Judea to Babylon, may without doubt suddenly in an hour bring the Apostles to thee. And wherefore doubtest thou

to see the wicked spirit, since thou hast
utterly broken his head, and hast de-
spoiled him from the empire of his
power? Nevertheless thy will be done,
that thou see not the fiend.'

And this said, the angel mounted into
heaven with great light, and the palm
shone by right great clearness, and was
like to a green rod whose leaves shone
like to the morrow star.

And it happed as St. John the Evangelist preached in Ephesus, the heaven
suddenly thundered, and a white cloud
took him up and brought him before the
gate of the blessed Virgin Mary. And
he knocked at the door and entered and
saluted the Virgin honourably.

Whom the blessed Virgin beheld, and
was greatly abashed for joy, and might
not abstain her from weeping, and said to
him :—'John, my son, remember thee of
the word of thy master, by which he made
me mother unto thee, and thee a son unto
me. Lo! I am called of thy master and
my God. I pay now the debt of human
condition, and recommend my body unto
thy busy cure. I have heard say that the
Jews have made a council, and said : Let
us abide brethren unto the time that she

that bare Jesus be dead, and then **incontinent** we shall take her body and shall cast it into the fire and burn it. Thou therefore take this palm, and bear it before the bier when ye shall bear my body to the sepulchre.'

Then said John:—'O would God that all my brethren the Apostles were here, that we might make thine exequies convenably as it behoveth and is dignified and worthy.'

And as he said that, all the Apostles were ravished with clouds from the places where they preached, and were brought before the door of the blessed Virgin Mary.

And when they saw them assembled, they marvelled, and said:—'For what cause hath our Lord assembled us here?'

Then St. John went out and said to them that our Lady should pass and depart out of this world, and added more thereto, saying:—'Brethren, beware and keep you from weeping when she shall depart, because that the people that shall see it be not troubled, and say: Lo! there, how they dread the death which preach to others the resurrection.'

F

And Denis, disciple of Paul, affirmeth
this same in the book of divine names,
that is to wit, that all the Apostles were
assembled at the Assumption and death
of our Lady Mary and were together
there, and that each of them made a sermon unto the praising and laud of Jesu
Christ and the blessed Virgin his mother.
He said thus, speaking to Timothy :—
'Thus we and thou, as thou well knowest,
and many of our holy brethren, did assemble at the vision of the mother that
received God.'

And James, brother of God, was there.
And Peter the Apostle, most noble and
sovereign of the theologians.

And after that me seemed that all
the Hierarchies lifted her up, after and
according to her virtue without end. This
saith St. Denis.

And when the blessed Virgin Mary saw
all the Apostles assembled, she blessed
our Lord, and sat in the midst of them
where the lamps, tapers, and lights burned.
And about the third hour of the night
Jesu Christ came with sweet melody and
song, with the orders of the angels, the
companies of patriarchs, the assembly of
martyrs, the convents of confessors, the

carols of virgins. And before the bed of
our blessed Lady the companies of all
these saints were set in order and made
sweet song and melody. And what exequies were done of our blessed Lady, and
there hallowed, it is all said and enseigned
in the foresaid book which is attributed to
St. John.

For first, Jesu Christ began to say:—
'Come my chosen and I shall set thee in
My seat, for I have coveted the beauty of
thee.' And our Lady answered:—'Sir,
my heart is ready'; and all they that
were come with Jesu Christ entuned
sweetly, saying:—'This is she that never
touched the bed of marriage in delight,
and she shall have fruit in refection of
holy souls.' Then she sang of herself,
saying:—'All the generations shall say that
I am blessed, for He that is mighty hath
done great things to me, and the name
of Him is holy.'

And the chanter of chanters entuned
more excellently above all others, saying:—'Come from Lebanon, my spouse,
come from Lebanon, come, thou shalt be
crowned.' And she said:—'I come, for
in the beginning of the book it is written
of me that I should do Thy will, for

my spirit hath joyed in Thee, God my
health.'

And thus in the morning the soul issued
out of the body and fled up in the arms
of her son.   And she was as far estranged
from the pain of the flesh as she was from
corruption of her body.

Then said our Lord to the Apostles :—
'Bear ye the body of this virgin, My
mother, into the vale of Jehosaphat and
lay ye her in a new sepulchre that ye shall
find there, and abide Me there three days
till that I return to you.'

And thereupon she was environed with
flowers of roses, that was the company of
martyrs, and with lilies of the valley, that
was the company of angels, of confessors
and virgins.

And the Apostles cried after her saying :—'Right wise virgin, whither goest
thou ?   Lady, remember thee of us.'

Then the company of saints that were
abiden there were awaked with the sound
of the song of them that mounted, and
came against her, and saw their King
bear in His proper arms the soul of a
woman, and saw that this soul was joined
to Him, and were abashed and began to
cry, saying :—'Who is this that ascendeth

from the desert, full of delices, joined to her friend?' And they that accompanied her said:—'This is the right fair among the daughters of Jerusalem, and like as ye have seen her full of charity and dilection, so is she joyously received, and set in the seat of glory on the right side of her son.'

And the Apostles saw the soul of her being so white that no mortal tongue might express it. And then three maidens that were there took off the clothes from the body for to wash it. The body there-upon shone by so great clearness that they might well feel it in touching and washing but they might not see it. And that light shone as long as they were about the washing of it.

Then the Apostles took the body honourably and laid it on the bier, and John said to Peter:—'Bear this palm before the bier, for our Lord hath ordained thee above us, and hath made thee pastor and prince of his sheep.' To whom Peter said:—'It appertaineth better to thee to bear it, for thou art chosen virgin of our Lord, and thou oughtest to bear this palm of light at the exequies of chastity and holiness, thou that drankest at the

fountain of perdurable clearness. And I
shall bear the holy body with the bier,
and these other Apostles our brethren
shall go round about the body yielding
thankings to God.' And then St. Paul
said to him :—'I, that am least of the
Apostles and of you all, shall bear with
thee.'

And then Peter and Paul lifted up the
bier, and Peter began to sing and say :—
'Israel is issued out of Egypt,' and the
other Apostles followed him in the same
song. And our Lord covered the bier
and the Apostles with a cloud, so that
they were not seen, but the voice of them
was heard only. And the angels were with
the Apostles singing, and replenished all
the land with marvellous sweetness.

Then all the people was moved with
that sweet melody, and issued hastily out
of the city and enquired what it was, and
then there were some that said to them
that Mary, such a woman is dead, and
the disciples of her son Jesu bear her
and make such melody as ye hear about
her.

And then ran they to arms, and they
warned each other, saying :—'Come and
let us slay all the disciples, and let us

burn the body of her that bare this traitor.'

And when the prince of priests saw that, he was all abashed and full of anger, and said :—'Lo ! here the tabernacle of Him that troubled us and our lineage. Behold what glory He now receiveth'; and in saying so, he laid his hands on the bier willing to turn it and overthrow it to the ground.

Then suddenly both his hands waxed dry and cleaved to the bier, so that he hung by the hands on the bier, and was sore tormented and wept and brayed. And the angels that were there in the clouds blinded all the other people that they saw nothing.

And the prince of priests said :—'St. Peter, despise me not in this tribulation, and I pray thee to pray for me to our Lord. Thou oughtest to remember when the chamberer, that was usher, accused thee, and I excused thee.' And St. Peter said to him :—'We be now engaged in the service of our Lady, and may not now hinder to heal thee, but and if thou believest in our Lord Jesu Christ, and in this that bare him, I ween and hope that thou soon shalt have health and be all

whole.' And he answered:—'I believe
our Lord Jesu Christ to be the Son of
God, and that this is his right holy
mother'; and thereupon his hands were
loosed from the bier, but yet the dryness
and the pain ceased not in him.

Then St. Peter said to him:—'Kiss
the bier and say: I believe in God Jesu
Christ that this woman bare in her belly,
and remained virgin after the childing.'
And when he had so said, he was immediately all whole perfectly. And then said
Peter to him:—'Take that palm of the
hand of our brother John, and lay it on
the people that be blind, and who that
will believe shall receive his sight again.
And they that will not believe shall never
see.'

And then the Apostles bare Mary unto
the monument and sat by it, like as our
Lord had commanded, and at the third
day Jesu Christ came with a great multitude of angels and saluted them, and
said:—'Peace be with you.' And they
answered:—'God, glory be to thee which
only makest the great miracles and mar-
vels.' And our Lord said to the Apostles:
'What is now your advice that I ought
now to do to my mother of honour and

of grace?' 'Sire, it seemeth to us Thy
servants that like as Thou hast vanquished
the death and reignest world without end,
that Thou raise also the body of Thy
mother and set it on Thy right side for
ever.' And He granted it.

Then Michael the angel came and pre-
sented the soul of Mary to our Lord.
And the Saviour spake and said :—'Arise
up, haste thee, my culver or dove, tabernacle of glory, vessel of life, temple
celestial, and like as thou never feltest
conceiving by none atouchment, thou
shalt not suffer by corruption of body in
the sepulchre.'

The soul came again to the body of
Mary, and issued gloriously out of the
tomb, and thus was received in the Heavenly chamber, and a great company of
angels with her.

And St. Thomas was not there, and
when he came he would not believe
this. And thereupon the girdle with
which her body was girt came to him
from the air, which he received, and
thereby he understood that she was
assumpt into Heaven.

All this heretofore is said and called
apocryphum. Whereof St. Jerome saith

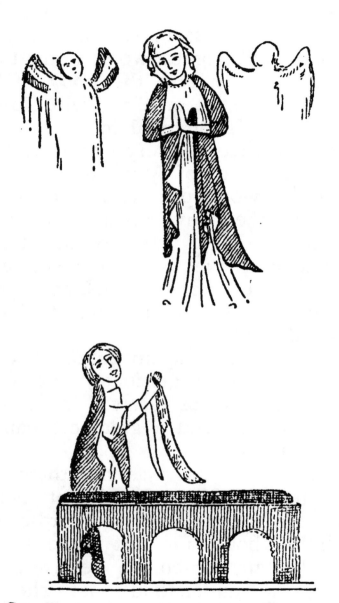

ST. THOMAS RECEIVES THE GIRDLE.
Mural Painting, Chalgrove, Oxon.

in a sermon to Paula and Eustochia her daughter :—' That book is said to be apocryphum, save that some words which be worthy of faith and be approved of saints as touching nine things, that is to wit, that the comfort of the Apostles was promised and given to the virgin, and that all the saints assembled there, and that she died without pain, and was buried in the vale of Jehosaphat.

And there were made ready the obsequies and the devotion of Jesu Christ, and the coming of the celestial company, and the persecution of the Jews, and the shining of the miracles, and that she was assumpt into Heaven, body and soul. But many other things be put there more at fantasy and simulation than at truth. As that, that Thomas was not there, and when he came he doubted, and other similar things, which be better not to believe them than not to believe her clothes and vestments were left in her tomb, to the comfort of good Christian men. And of one part of her vestments it is said that there happed such a great miracle as followeth.

When the Duke of Normandy had besieged the city of Chartres, the bishop of

the city took the coat of our Lady and set
it on the head of a spear like a banner
and went out against the enemy surely,
and the people followed him.   And immediately all the host of the enemies were
turned into frenzy, and were blind and
trembled, and all were abashed.   And
when they of the city saw this thing,
above the divine demonstrance they went
on eagerly and slew their enemies, the
which thing displeased much the Virgin
St. Mary, as it was proved by that that
her coat vanished away, and the duke,
their enemy, found it in his lap.

It is read in the revelations of St. Elizabeth that, on a time as she was ravished
in spirit, she saw in a place much far from
folk a tomb or a sepulchre environed with
much light, and was like the form of a
woman within, and there was about it
a great multitude of angels, and a little
while after she was taken out of the
sepulchre and borne up on high with that
multitude.   And then came against her a
man bearing in his right arm the sign of
the cross, and had with him many angels
without number, which received her very
joyously and led her with great melody
into Heaven.

And a little while after, Elizabeth demanded of an angel to whom she spake oft, of that vision that she saw. 'It is showed to thee,' said the angel, 'in that vision that the Virgin our Lady is assumpt into Heaven as well in her body as in her soul.'

It is said in the same revelations that it was showed to her that the fortieth day after the soul departed from her body she was so assumpt into Heaven, and also that when our blessed Lady spake to her, she said:—'After the Ascension of our Lord a whole year, and as many days more as be from the Ascension unto her assumption, she overlived.' And also she said:—'All the Apostles were at my departing, and buried my body honourably, and forty days after was raised.' And then St. Elizabeth demanded of her whether she should hide this thing, or that she should manifest it and show it. And she said:—'It is not to be showed to fleshly nor unbelieving people, but it is not to be hid to devout and Christian people.'

It is to be noted that the glorious Virgin Mary was assumpt and lifted up into Heaven entirely joyously and gloriously. She was received entirely, that is,

wholly, as the Church believeth, and that
many saints affirm, and enforce them to
prove it by many reasons.   And the reason
of St. Bernard is such.   He saith that God
hath made the body of St. Peter and St.
James so gloriously to be honoured that
He hath enhanced them by marvellous
honour, that to them is given a place
worthy for to be worshipped, which all
the world goeth to seek and offer to
them.

Then if the body of His blessed mother
were on the earth, and not haunted by devout visitation of Christian men, it should
be a marvel to hear that God would not
have done as much worship to His mother,
and honoured her body as much as the
bodies of other saints upon the earth.
Jerome saith thus, that the Virgin Mary
mounted into Heaven the eighteenth ca-
lends of September.   That which he saith
of the Assumption of the body of Mary,
the Church will rather believe than rashly
to explain it, and he proved it afterward
that it is to be believed that they that
arose with our Lord have accomplished
their eternal resurrection. Wherefore should
not we say then that it is done in the
Blessed Virgin Mary.

Many believe that St. John the Evangelist is glorified in his flesh with Jesu Christ; and then much more our Lady ought to be glorified in Heaven, both body and soul, which saith :—'Worship thy father and mother, and he came not to break the law but to fulfil it,' and therefore He honoureth his mother above all other.

St. Austin affirmeth not this only, but he proveth it by three reasons. And the first reason is the unity and assembly of the flesh of our Lord and of our Lady, and saith thus:—'Putrefaction and worms is the reproach of the human condition, which Jesu never touched, and the flesh of Jesu is out of this reproof, the nature of Mary is out thereof, for it is proved that Jesu Christ hath taken His flesh of her. The second reason is the dignity of the body of her of whom himself saith :—'This is the siege of God, the chamber of our Lord of heaven, and the tabernacle of Christ.' She is worthy to be where He is, so precious a treasure is more worthy to be kept in heaven than in earth. The third reason is perfect entireness of her virginal flesh, and saith thus:—'Enjoy thou Mary of honourable gladness in body and

in soul.   In thy proper son, and by thy
proper son, thou oughtest to have no harm
of corruption; where thou haddest no corruption of virginity in childing so great a
son, so thou whom He endued with so
great glory shouldst be alway without corruption, and live entirely, which barest
entire Him that is perfect of all, and that
she be with Him whom she bare in her
womb, and that she be at Him whom she
childed, gave suck and nourished.   Mary,
mother of Jesu Christ, administress and
servant.'   And because I may feel none
other thing, I dare not otherwise say
nor presume.   And hereof saith a noble
versifier :—

Transit ad æthera, virgo puerpera, virgula Jesse,
Non sine corpory, sed sine tempore, tendit adesse.

The virgin that childed mounted into
Heaven, the little rod of Jesse, not without body, but without time, she entendeth
to be there, virgin pure and net.

Secondly, she was assumpt and taken
up gladly.   And hereof saith Gerard,
bishop and martyr, in his homily :—'The
heavens received this day the Blessed
Virgin, the angels were glad, the archangels enjoyed, the thrones sang, the

dominations made melody, the principalities harmonised, the powers harped,
cherubim and seraphim sang laudings and
praisings, and bringing her with thankings
and lauds unto the siege of the divine
and sovereign majesty.'

Thirdly, she was lifted up in Heaven
so honourably that, Jesu Christ himself,
with all the strength of the heavenly company, came against her. Of whom St.
Jerome saith :—'Who is he that is suffi-
cient to think how the glorious queen of
the world went up this day, and how the
multitude of the celestial legions came
against her with great talent of devotion,
and with what songs she was brought unto
her seat, and how she was received of her
son and embraced with peaceable cheer
and clear face, and how she was enhanced
above all other creatures?' And yet he
saith:—'It is on this day that the chivalry
of Heaven came hastily for to meet
with the mother of God, and environed
her with great light, and brought her
to her seat with praisings and songs
spiritual.'

And then enjoyed them the celestial
company of Jerusalem with so great gladness that no man may recount nor tell,

and made joy and song, all enjoying in
charity because that this feast is every
year hallowed of us, and made continuous
with all others.

And it is to believe that the Saviour
Himself came and met with her hastily,
and brought her with Him, and set her in
her seat with great joy.   And how had
He accomplished otherwise that which
He commanded in the law, saying :—
'Honour thy father and mother.'

Fourthly, she was received excellently.
St. Jerome saith :—'This is the day in
which the Virgin Mary, not corrupt, went
unto the highness of the throne, and she
was there enhanced in the heavenly king-
dom and honoured gloriously, sitting next
unto Christ.'   And how she is enhanced
in the heavenly glory, Gerard the bishop
rehearseth in his homilies, saying :—' Our
Lord Jesu Christ alone may praise this
blessed Virgin His mother as He did, and
magnify, so that she be continually praised
of that Majesty, and honoured and environed of the company of angels, enclosed
with the assembly of archangels, possessed
of the thrones and girt about of the dominations, environe d with the service of the
powers, beclipped with the embracements

of the principalities, enjoyed with the
honours of the virtues, obeyed with lauds
and praisings of the cherubims, and possessed on all parts with not recountable
songs of the seraphims.' And the over
great and ineffable Trinity enjoyeth in
her eternal gladness, and His grace re-
doundeth all in her and maketh all other
to entend and await on her. The over-
shining order of the Apostles honour her
with ineffable laud. The honourable
multitude of martyrs beseech her in all
manner as one so great a lady. The
fellowship of confessors innumerable con-
tinue their song to her, the right noble
and white company of virgins make noble
carolling of the glory of her. Hell, full
of malice, howleth, and the cursed devils
cry unto her and dread her.

There was a clerk, devout unto the
Virgin Mary, which studied every day
how he might comfort her against the
pain of the five wounds of Jesu Christ,
saying thus :—' Rejoice thee virgin and
mother undefiled, which receives the joy
of the angels, enjoy that thou conceivedst,
enjoy thee that childedst the light of clearness, enjoy thee mother which never wert
touched, all features and all creatures

praise thee mother of light, be thou for us always praying to our Lord.' And as this clerk had lain long with an over great sickness, and came toward his end, he began to dread, and was troubled, and our blessed Lady appeared to him and said :—'Son, wherefore tremblest thou by so great fear, which hast so oft showed to me joy? Be thou joyful now thyself, and that thou mayest enjoy eternity, come with me.'

There was a monk much jolly and light of his living but devout to our Lady, which on a night went to do his accustomed folly; but when he passed before the altar of our lady, he saluted the virgin, and so went forth out of the church. And as he should pass a river he fell into the water and drowned, and the devils took the soul. Then came angels for to deliver it, and the devils said to them :—'Wherefore come ye hither? Ye have nothing in this soul.' And anon the blessed Virgin came, and blamed them because they had taken the soul which was hers. And they said that they had found him finishing his life in evil works. And she said :—'It is false that ye say, I know well that when he went into any place he saluted me first, and when he returned and came again also; and if ye say that I do you wrong, let us put it again in judgment of the Sovereign King.' And when they strove before our Lord of this matter, it pleased Him that the soul should return again to the body and repent him of his sins and trespasses. And then the brethren saw that the Matins were over long deferred, and sought the sexton, and went to the river and found him there drowned. And when they had drawn the body out of the water what they should do they wist not, and marvelled what he had done; and suddenly he came again to life, and told what he had done, and after finished his life in good works.

There was a knight which was mighty and rich, that foolishly dispended his goods, and came to so great a poverty that he which had been accustomed to give largely great things, had need to demand and ask the small. And he had a right chaste wife, and much devout to the blessed Virgin Mary. And a great solemnity approached, at which the knight was accustomed to give many gifts. And he had nothing to give, whereof he was greatly ashamed. And he went into a desert place full of heaviness, and of weeping, until the feast was past, to wail there his evil fortune and to hide his shame. And thereupon a knight, very horrible, came, sitting on an horse, which reasoned with the knight and enquired of him the cause of his great heaviness. And he told him all by order that as was happed to him. And this foul knight said to him :—'If thou wilt a little obey to me, thou shalt abound in glory and in riches more than thou wert before.' And he promised to the devil that he would do so gladly if he accomplished that he promised. And then he said to him :— 'Go home into thine house, and thou shalt find in such a place there, so much gold and so much silver. And thou shalt find there also precious stones, and so arrange that on such a day thou bring me hither thy wife.' And the knight returned home into his house, and found all things like as the devil had promised.

In course of time he bought a palace and gave great gifts, and bought again his heritage, and took his men again to him. And the day approached which he had promised to lead his wife to the fiend, and called her, saying:—'Let us go to horseback, for ye must come with me unto a place far hence.' And she trembled and was afeard, and durst not gainsay the commandment of her husband. And she commended herself devoutly to the blessed Virgin, and began to ride after her husband.

And when they had ridden a good while they saw in the way a church, and she descended from the horse and entered into the church. Her husband abode without. And as she commended herself devoutly to the blessed Virgin Mary in great devotion and contemplation, she suddenly slept, and the glorious Virgin put on a dress resembling the habit of this lady and departed from the altar and issued out and mounted upon the horse. And the lady abode sleeping in the church, and the knight weened that she had been his wife that was with him, and went on his way.

And when he was come to the place assigned, the devil came with a great noise to the place, and when he approached and came near, he quaked and trembled anon and durst go no nearer. Then said he to the knight:—'Thou most traitor of all

men, wherefore hast thou deceived me,
and hast rendered to me harm for such
great good as I have given to thee? I
said to thee that thou shouldst bring thy
wife to me, and thou hast brought the
mother of God. I would have thy wife,
and thou hast brought to me Mary. For
thy wife hath done to me many injuries,
wherefore I would take on her vengeance.
And thou hast brought to me this for to
torment me, and for to send me to
hell.

When the knight heard this he was sore
abashed, and might not hold him from
weeping, and durst not speak for dread
and marvel. And then the Blessed Mary
said :—' Thou felon spirit, by what folly
dost thou will to grieve and annoy my
devout servant? This shall not be left in
thee unpunished. I bind thee in this
sentence, that thou descend into hell,
and that thou henceforth have no pre-
sumption to grieve none that call upon
me.' And then he went away with great
howling.

And the man sprang down from his
horse and kneeled down on his knees to
her feet. And the Virgin our Lady blamed
him, and commanded him to return again

to his wife, which yet slept in the church, and bade him that he should cast away, all the riches of the devil. And when he came again he found his wife yet sleeping, and awoke her, and told to her all that was befallen. And when they were come home they threw away all the riches of the devil, and dwelled alway in the love of our Lady, and received afterward many riches that our Lady gave to them.

There was a man which was ravished in judgment before God, for he had much sinned, and the devil was there and said :—'Ye have nothing on this soul, but it ought to be mine, for I have thereof a public document.' To whom our Lord said :—'Where is thine instrument?' 'I have,' he said, 'an instrument that thou saidest with thy proper mouth and hast ordained it for to endure perpetually. For thou saidest in what hour that ye eat of it ye shall die, and this is of the lineage of them that took of the meat forbidden. And by right of this public instrument he ought to be judged to me.' And then our Lord said :—'Let the man speak'; but the man spake not. And the devil said yet again :—'The soul is mine, for if he hath done any good deeds, the wicked deeds pass the good without comparison.' And then our Lord would not give sentence against him, but He gave him a term of eight days, so that at the end of eight days he should appear again before Him, and give account of all these things.

And as he went from the face of our Lord, sorrowing and trembling, he met with a man which asked the cause of his heaviness. And he told to him all by order, and he said to him :—'Doubt thee nothing, and be not afraid, for I shall help thee manly from the first.' And he demanded of him his name, and he said :—'Verity.' And after he found another which promised to help him. And when he had asked his name, he said his name was 'Righteousness.'

At the eighth day he came to the doom before the judge, and the devil opposed to him the first case, and Truth answered and said :—'We know well that there is double death, corporal and infernal, and this instrument that the devil allegeth against thee speaketh no word of the death of hell, but of the death of the body, and of that it is clear that all men be enclosed in that sentence, that is to wit, that he dieth in his body, and that is not the death of hell. And as touching the death of the body, the sentence endureth always, but as to the death of the soul, it is repealed by the death of Jesu Christ.'

Then the devil saw that he was discharged of the first. Then he opposed and alleged the second, but Righteousness came and answered thus :—' Howbeit that he hath been thy servant many years, nevertheless reason gainsayeth it. For reason murmured always because he served so cruel a lord.'

But at the third objection, he had no help, and our Lord said:—'Bring forth the balance, and let all the good and evil be weighed.' Then Truth and Righteousness said to the sinner:—'Run with all thy thought unto the Lady of mercy which sitteth by the judge and study to call her to thine help.' And when he had so done, the blessed Virgin Mary came in to his help and laid her hand upon the balance whereas were but few good deeds. And the devil enforced him to draw on that other side, but the mother of mercy won and obtained and delivered the sinner.

And then he came again to himself and amended his life.

It happed in the city of Bourges, about the year of our Lord five hundred and twenty-seven, that when the Christian men were communed and houseled on an Easter day, a child of a Jew went to the altar with the other children, and received our Lord's body with the others. And when he came home, his father demanded him whence he came, and he answered that he came from school, and that he had been houseled with them at Mass. And then the father, full of madness, took the child and threw him into a burning furnace that was there. And thereupon the mother of God came in the form of an image, which the child had seen standing on the altar, and kept him from the fire without taking any harm.

The mother of the child, with her great crying, made to assemble many Christian men and Jews, who saw the child in the furnace without any harm or hurt, and they drew him out, and demanded him how he escaped, and he answered and said:—'That reverend lady which stood upon the altar came and helped me, and put away all the fire from me.'

Then the Christian men, understanding this to be the image of our Lady, took the father of the child and threw him into the furnace, and immediately he was burnt and consumed.

On one occasion, before daybreak, there were certain monks standing by a river, who talked and wrangled there of fables and idle words. And they heard a great rowing, and oars beating the water coming hastily. And the monks asked :—'Who be ye?' And they said :—'We be devils that bear to hell the soul of Ebronien, provost of the house of the king of France, which was apostate in the monastery of St. Gall.' And when the monks heard that they doubted strongly, and cried high:—'St. Mary, pray for us!' And the devils said :—'Well have ye called Mary, for we would have separated you and drowned you because of your dissolute and untimely wrangling.' And then the monks returned to their convent, and the devils went in to hell.

There was a woman that suffered many griefs and injuries of a devil which appeared visibly to her in the form of a man, and she sought many remedies, now holy water, now one thing, now another, but he ceased not. And then a holy man counselled her that, when he came to her that she should lift up her hands to heaven and cry :—'St. Mary, help me!' And when she had so done, the devil fled all afraid as though he had been smitten with a stone, and afterwards he stood and said :—'The cursed devil enter into his mouth that taught thee that prayer, and immediately he vanished away and never came again.'

Here followeth yet of the Assumption of our Blessed Lady.

The manner of the Assumption of the right holy Virgin Mary is showed in a sermon made and ordained of divers sayings of saints, the which is read solemnly in many churches, and therein is contained all that I can find in the world, in narrations of holy fathers, of the departing out of this life of the glorious Virgin Mary, mother of God, that I have set here to the loving and praising of her.

St. Cosmo, which had to surname Vestitor, saith he hath learned of his foregoers that which ought not to be forgotten, and saith that Jesu Christ ordained and disposed the life of his mother to be finished. He sent an angel which showed to her before the announcing of her departing, that death should not come **suddenly or give** her tribulation. And she had prayed him, her son, face to face, when he was here in earth, that she should not see any wicked spirit. He sent then to her the angel with these words :—'It is time to take My mother with Me and thus as thou hast replenished the earth with joy, so make heaven to enjoy. Thou shalt render the mansions of My father joyous. And thou shalt comfort the spirits of My saints. Be not thou wroth to leave the corruptible world with its selfishness, but take the celestal palace. Mother, be not afraid to be taken from thy flesh, thou that art called to the life eternal, to joy without failing, to the rest of peace, to sure conversation, to refection not recordable, to light not quenchable, to day not evening, to glory not recountable, to Myself, thy son, Maker of all things, for I am Life Eternal, love not corruptible, habitation not recordable, light without darkness, bounty not estimable. Give to the earth without trembling that which is his. None shall ravish thee out of Mine hands, for in My hands be all the ends of the world ; deliver to Me thy body, for I have put in thee My Deity or Godhead. The death shall never have joy on thee, for thou hast borne the very light ; neither breaking or destruction shall environ thee, for thou hast deserved to be My vessel. Come thou thereupon to Him which is born of thee for to receive the guerdons of the womb of the mother, and the reward of thy milk for My meat. Come now fast, and haste thee to join thee to Me, thine only son. I know well thou shalt not be constrained for the love of another son rather than of Me that showeth thee virgin and mother. I show thee a wall of steadfast faith, thou art an arch of salvation, a bridge to them that fleet, a staff to the feeble, a ladder to them that go up and mount to Heaven, the most gentle advocate for sinners. I shall bring the Apostles to thee, of whom thou shalt be buried right of their hands, for it appertaineth to My spiritual children of light, to whom I have given the Holy Ghost to bury thy body, and that they accomplish in thy person the service of thy marvellous departing out of the earth.'

After the angel had recounted these things, he gave to our Lady a bough of palm, sent from the plant of Paradise, in token of the victory against the corruption of death and clothes of immortality, and when he had said this, he ascended up into Heaven from whence he came from.

Then the blessed Virgin Mary assembled her neighbours and said to them :— 'I let you wit certainly that I am at the end of my temporal life, and shall hastily depart ; wherefore it behoveth that ye wake, for to every each that shall pass out of this world, good angels and wicked spirits gladly come.' And when they heard this they began to weep and say :—'Thou doubtest the sight of the spirits, who hast deserved to be mother of the Maker of all things, and barest Him that robbed hell, which hast deserved to have the seat above Cherubim and Seraphim, how shall we do then? And whither shall we flee ?'

And there were a great multitude of women weeping, and said that she should not leave them orphans. And the blessed Virgin, our Lady, said in comforting them :—'Ye that be mothers of corruptible

H

sons, may not well suffer to be a little while thence from your children, how then ought not I to desire to go to my son, which am mother and virgin, and he is only son of God the Father. And if ye or any of ye had but one son, ye would desire to see him and be comforted in the lineage of him, and I then, that am not corrupt, wherefore should not I be desirous to see Him which is life of all creatures?'

And whilst they spake these things, the blessed St. John, the Evangelist, came and inquired how the matter went, and then when our Lady had told to him of her hasty departing, he fell down stretched to the earth, and said, with weeping tears:—'O Lord, what be we? Wherefore sendest Thou to us so many tribulations? Why hast Thou not ere this taken away the soul from my body, and that I had been better visited by Thy blessed mother, than I should come to her departing?' And then the blessed Virgin led him weeping into her chamber, and showed to him the palm and the vestments which the angel had brought, and after, laid her down in her bed for to be there till her passing.

And immediately after came a great noise of thunder, and a whirlwind brought a cloud whiter than snow, in which the Apostles were brought before the gate of our blessed Lady, like as it had rained, so fell they down one after another. And as they marvelled of this thing, John came to them and told to them what the angel had showed to our Lady.

And then they all wept and St. John comforted them, and then they dried their eyes and entered in to the blessed Virgin, and saluted her honourably and adored, and she said to them :—'My dear children, God, my son, keep you all.' And when they had told to her of their coming, she greeted them all in their turn. And the Apostles said :—'Right honourable Lady and Virgin, we, in beholding thee, be greatly comforted, like as we should be in our Lord and Master, and we have only comfort in ourselves because we hope that thou shalt be mediatrix for us unto God.' And then she saluted Paul by name :—'God save thee, expositor of my comfort, howbeit that thou hast not seen Jesu Christ in his flesh.' 'Nevertheless I am comforted' said St. Paul, 'that I may see thee in the flesh. And unto this day I have preached to the people that thou hast borne Jesu Christ. And now I shall preach that thou art borne up to Heaven to Him.' And after, the Virgin showed to him that which the angel had brought, and warned them that the lights should not be put out till that she were departed, and there were two hundred and twenty tapers.

And then she clad her with the cloth of mortality and saluted them all, and ordained her body to abide in her bed unto her issue and departing. And Peter stood at the head, and John at the feet, and the other Apostles were about the bed, and gave laud to the virgin mother of God.

Then Peter began the song and said :— 'Enjoy thou spouse of God in the chambers celestial, thou candlestick of light without darkness, by thee is showed the everlasting light and clearness.'

The blessed Archbishop of Constantinople witnesseth that all the Apostles were assembled at the passing of the blessed Virgin Mary, the right sweet mother of God, saying thus :—'Blessed

Lady, mother of God, thou that hast received of the human nature the death
which may not be eschewed, yet shalt
thou not sleep, and the eye shall not
slumber that keepeth thee. Thy departing hence nor thy falling asleep shall
not be without witness. The heavens
recount the glory of them that sang
over thee in earth, and of them shall
the truth be showed. The clouds cry
to thee honour, and to Him that minis-
tereth to thee. The angels shall preach
the service of life done in thee by the
Apostles which were assembled with thee
in Jerusalem.'

And St. Denis, Areopagite, witnesseth
the same, saying :—'We, as I know well,
and they and many of our brethren, were
assembled for to see the body of her that
bare God. And James, the brother of
God, and Peter, the right noble and sovereign of theologians, were present. And
after, it pleased them that, after this vision,
all the sovereign priests sang praises after
each of them had conceived in his thought
of the bounty of her.'

St. Cosmo, in following the narration,
saith :—'And after this a great thunder
knocked at the house with so great an

odour of sweetness, that with the sweet
spirit the house was replenished, in such
wise that all they that were there save the
Apostles, and three virgins which held the
lights, slept.   Then our Lord came with
a great multitude of angels and took the
soul of His mother, and the soul of her
shone by so great light that none of the
Apostles might behold it.   And our Lord
said to St. Peter :—' Bury the corpse of
My mother with great reverence, and
keep it there three days diligently, and
I shall then come again, and transport
her unto Heaven without corruption, and
shall clothe her of the semblable clearness of Myself; that which I have taken
of her, and that which she hath taken
of Me, shall be assembled together and
accord.'

That same St. Cosmo rehearseth a dread-
ful and marvellous mystery of natural dis-
sention and of curious inquisition.   For
all things that be said of the glorious
Virgin, mother of God, be marvellous
above nature and be more to doubt than
to enquire.   For when the soul was issued
out of the body, the body said these
words :—' Sire, I thank Thee that I am
worthy of Thy grace ; remember Thee

of me, for I am but a weak thing, and have kept that which thou deliveredst me.'

And then the other awoke and saw the body of the Virgin without soul, and then began strongly to weep and were heavy and sorrowful.

And then the Apostles took up the body of the blessed Virgin and bare it to the monument, and St. Peter began the psalm :—*In exitu Israel de Egypto,* and then the companies of angels gave laudings and praisings to the Virgin in such wise that all Jerusalem was moved for that great joy, so that the sovereign priests sent great multitude of people with glaives and staves, and one of them, in a great fury, came to the bier and would have thrown it down with the body of the blessed mother of God. And because that he enforced him so maliciously to touch and draw down the corpse, he lost his hands by his deserving, for both his hands were cut off by the wrists and hung on the bier, and he was tormented by horrible sorrow, and he required pardon and promised amends. St. Peter said to him :—'Thou mayest in no wise have pardon if thou kiss not the bier of the blessed Virgin, and that thou confess also

Jesu Christ the Son of God to be formed
in her.' And then, when he had so done,
his hands were joined again to his wrists,
and was all whole.

THE VIRGIN'S BIER.
Sculpture, Notre Dame, Paris.

Then St. Peter took a leaf of the palm
and gave it to him and said :—' Go in to
the city and lay it on them that be sick,
and they that will believe shall receive
health.'

And then when the Apostles came to
the Vale of Jehosaphat, they found a

sepulchre like unto the sepulchre of our Lord, and laid therein the body with great reverence, but they durst not touch it, which was the right holy vessel of God, but the sudary in which she was wrapped, and laid it in the sepulchre.

And as the Apostles were about the sepulchre after the commandment of our Lord, at the third day, a cloud much bright environed the sepulchre, and the voice of angels was heard sound sweetly and a marvellous odour was felt sweet smelling. And when our Lord was come and seen descending there, all were marvellously abashed, and He bare the body with Him of the blessed Virgin with much great glory.

Then the Apostles kissed the sepulchre and returned into the house of St. John Evangelist, praising him as keeper and guard of so noble a virgin.

And one of the Apostles failed at this great solemnity, and when he heard so great miracles, he marvelled and required with great desire that her sepulchre might be opened for to know the truth of all these things. And the Apostles denied it to him. All said that the witness of so great persons ought to suffice, to

the end that lest peradventure the mis-
believed men should say that the body
were stolen away or drawn by theft.
And he then, which was angry, said :—
'Why defend ye to me that which am
one with you in your common treasures?'
And at the last they opened the sepulchre and found not the body, but they
found only but the vestments, and the
sudary.

St. Germain, Archbishop of Constantinople, saith that he found written in the
History Euthimiata in the third book of
the fortieth chapter, and the same witnesseth the great Damascene, that as the
noble empress Helen in mind of Holy
Church had made many churches in
Constantinople, among all other she edi-
fied in the time of Marcian the emperor
at Balthernas a marvellous church in the
honour of the Virgin Mary, and called
Juvenal, Archbishop of Jerusalem, and all
the other bishops of Palestine which
dwelled then in the city royal for the
Council which had been holden in
Chalcedon, and she said to them :—
'We have heard say that the body of
the right holy Virgin our Lady is in such
a place, in such a tomb in the Vale of

Jehosaphat ; we will then that for the guard of this city, that the body of the blessed Virgin be transported hither with due honour and reverence. And Juvenal answered to her, like as he had found in ancient histories, that the body was borne into glory, and was not in the monument, for there was nothing left but the vestments and the sudary only. And those vestments Juvenal sent then into Constantinople, and were there laid honourably.

And let no man ween that I have made this of my proper head and engine, but I have set it here which 'I have by doctrine and study learned of the lesson of them, which by tradition and learning of their foregoers have received it. And hitherto endure the words of the said sermon.

Yet of the Assumption of our Blessed Lady.

Verily John Damascene, which for the time was a Greek, saith many marvellous things of the Assumption of the right holy and glorious Virgin Mary. For he saith in his sermons that, this day the right holy and

sumptuous ark which bare within her her
maker was brought and set in the temple
which was not made of hands. On this
day the right holy culver or dove, innocent and simple, fled from the ark, that
is to say from the body in which God
received and found rest.

On this day the Virgin that conceived,
not knowing earthly passions, but induced
by celestial intentions shall not fail, but
shall be called very heaven, soul dwelling
in the celestial tabernacles. And howbeit
that the right holy soul be separate from
her blessed body, and that her body was
laïd in the sepulchre, nevertheless it is not
dead, nor shall be corrupt by rotting, that
is to wit, the body of whom, childing, the
virginity remained without any hurting or
dissolution, and is transported to better
and more holy life without corruption
of death for to remain in the eternal
tabernacles.

And like as the sun shining clear at
other times, is hid, and appeareth failing
a short time, yet she hath lost nothing of
her light, but in herself is the fountain of
eternal light.

Thou art the fountain of light without
wasting, the treasure of life, howbeit that

by short interval or space of time thou shalt be brought to corporal death, nevertheless thou givest to us, abundantly, clearness of light without default, and thy holy dormition, or sleeping, is not called death, but a passing or departing, or more properly a coming, for thou, departing from the body camest to Heaven, and Jesu Christ, angels and archangels, and all the heavenly company came to meet thee.

The foul and damned spirits doubt much thy noble and excellent coming, and thou, blessed and glorious Virgin thou wentest not to Heaven as did Elijah, and thou mountedst not as Paul did unto the third heaven only, but thou camest and touchedst the siege royal of thy son.

The death of other saints may well be said death, for that death maketh them blessed, but he hath no place in thee. For thy death or thy transmigration or thy perfection, or thy departing, giveth thee no surety to be blessed; for thou art the beginning, middle, and end of all weals and goods, which exceed human thought. Thy surety, thy very perfection, and thy conception without seed, and thy divine habitation have made thee blessed ; whereof thou saidest thyself that, thou art not made blessed by thy death, but of thy conception, in all generations.   And death hath not made thee blessed, but thou hast ennoblished the death in taking away the heaviness and sorrow thereof, converting it into joy.   For God said : Lest peradventure the first form of man, that is to wit Adam, put forth his hand, and take of the Tree of Life, and live for ever, how then shall not she live in Heaven eternally that bare this life which is eternal and without end?

Sometime God putteth out of Paradise the first parents which slept in the death of sin, buried from the beginning of inobedience and gluttony, and now she that hath borne life to all human lineage, and was obedient to God the Father, and put away from her all odour of sin, how shall not she be in Heaven ? Wherefore should not she enjoy the gates of Heaven?   Eve stretched her ear to the serpent, of whom she took the mortal venom, and because she did it for delight, she was subdued to bearing and bringing forth children in sorrow and pain, and was condemned with Adam.

But this blessed Virgin that inclined her ear to the word of God, whom the Holy Ghost replenished, which bare in her womb the mercy of the Father; which conceived without knowledge of man, and childed without pain and sorrow, how durst death swallow her? How might anything have corruption that bare life.

And yet saith the said Damascene in his sermons :—'Verily the Apostles were departed through the world in all countries and entended to preaching to men, and to draw them out of the deep darkness by one holy word, and brought them to the celestial table and to the solemn espousals of God. And then the divine commandment, which is a net or cloud, brought them from all the parts of the world into Jerusalem, in assembling them between his wings. And then Adam and Eve our first parents cried :—Come to us, right holy and wholesome refuge, which fulfillest our desire. And the company of saints which was there, said again :— Remain with us our comfort and leave us not orphans, thou art the comfort of our travails, refreshing of our sweatings, that if thou · live it is to us a glorious thing to live with thee, and if thou die, it is glorious to us to die with thee. How should we be in this life, and shall be destitute of the presence of thy life.

And, as I suppose, such things and similar said the Apostles with great plenty of them of the Church, with great wailings and sighs in complaining them from the departing. And she, returning towards her son, said :—'Sire, I pray Thee to be very comforter to my sons whom it pleased Thee to call brethren, which be heavy and sorrowful of my departing. And with that I shall bless them with my hand, give to them Thy blessing upon my blessing.'

And then she stretched out her hand, and blessed all the college of good Christian men, and then said after :— 'Lord, I commend my spirit into Thy hands, receive my soul, Thy love, which Thou hast kept without blame of sin to Thyself. And I commend my body to the earth for to keep it whole, or where it shall please Thee to enhabit it, transport me to Thee, so where Thou art the infantment or fruit of my womb that I be dwelling with Thee.' All these words heard the Apostles.

Then said our Lord :—'Arise up, My beloved, and come to Me. O thou most fair among women, My love, thou art fair, and no spot of filth is in thee.'

And when the right blessed Virgin heard that, she commended her spirit into the hands of her son. Then the Apostles were bedewed with tears, and kissed the tabernacle. And by the blessing and holiness of the holy body, whosoever touched the bier devoutly were healed of whatsoever sickness they had. Devils were chased from demoniacs, the air and the heaven were purified by the assumption of the soul, and the earth by the deposition of the body. And the water was sanctified by the washing of the body. For the body was washed with right holy water and clean. And the holy body was not made clean by the water, but the water was hallowed of her.

And after, the holy body was wounden and wrapped in a clean sudary, and was laid upon the bed, and lamps burnt full bright about her. Ointments gave a great and fragrant odour, the laudings and praisings of angels resounded. And the Apostles and other that were there sang divine songs.

And the ark of our Lord was borne in to Mount of Sion, unto the Vale of Jehosaphat, upon the heads of the Apostles. And the angels went before, and some followed the body, and other conveyed her. And she was accompanied of all the multitude of the Church.

And some of the Jews who heard it, in their evil malice descended down from the Mount of Sion, and one of them, which was a member of the devil, ran foolishly unto the holy body, and assailed it for to have cast it to the earth, drawing it with both his hands, and both his hands cleaved to the bier, and were departed from the body, like as two staves had been sawed off, and so he was like a trunk till that faith changed his thought. And he wailing so ruefully repented him, and they that bare the bier tarried, and made that Jew worship and touch the holy body, and then came his hands again into their first estate, and then was the body borne unto the Vale of Jehosaphat, and there it was embraced and kissed, and songs sung of holy laudings and praisings, and there were wept many tears, and then the holy body was laid in the tomb honourably, but her soul was not left in hell, nor her flesh never felt corruption.

And they said that she was the well which never was digged, the field not eared, the vine not cut, the olive bearing fruit which shall not be holden in the bosom of the earth. For it appertaineth that the mother be enhanced with the son. And that she mount to Him, like as He descended in to her. And that she that hath kept her virginity in her childing ought to see no corruption. And she that bare the Creator of all the world in her belly ought to dwell in divine tabernacles. And that she whom the Father had taken to espouse, were kept in the celestial chambers. And those things that belong to the son, ought to be possessed of the mother. And all this saith John Damascene.

Yet of the Assumption of our Lady, after St. Austin.

St. Austin showeth authentically in a sermon of the right holy Assumption of our blessed Lady, saying :—'We that have begun to speak of the body of the eternal Virgin, and of the Assumption of her blessed soul, we say thus :—first, that we find nothing of her written since that our Lord hanging on the cross commended her to his disciple, save that Luke recordeth in his writings, saying that all they were by one courage persevering with the Virgin Mary, mother of our Lord Jesu Christ. What is then to say of her death, and of her Assumption? Whereof the Scripture remembereth nothing, it is then as meseemeth to be enquired, what thing which is according to truth, without which authority is nothing. We remember the human condition : we doubt not to say that surely she went to temporal death. And if we say that she is resolved into common putrefaction in worms and into ashes or dust it behoveth us to weigh and think such thing as appertaineth to so great holiness, and to the lordship of such a chamber of God.

We know well that it was said to the first father :—Thou art powder, and into powder thou shalt return; but the flesh of Jesu Christ escaped from this condition, for his flesh suffered never corruption. Then is exempt from this general sentence the nature taken of the Virgin.

And God said to the woman Eve :—' I shall multiply thy diseases and thou shalt bring forth children with pain and sorrow.' But Mary suffered never such diseases, of whom the sword 'of sorrow pierced the soul. But Mary childed without sorrow. And then if she were quit, and had no part of sorrow in childing, then ought she not to have part of diseases, nor of corruption.

But she is exempt from some other generalities, because the dignity gave to her such lordship. And though we say that she suffered death, yet is she not retained with the bonds of death.

If our Lord would keep His mother entire and whole, and the chastity of her virginity, wherefore may He not keep without corruption, of stench, of rottenness? It appertaineth then to the honour of our Lord, to keep the honour of His mother which was not come to break the law, but to accomplish it, and in His life had worshipped her before all others by the grace of her conceiving.

Therefore we ought well to believe that He honoureth her at her death with singular salvation, and of special grace. And rottenness and worms be but reproach of human condition. And when Jesu Christ is out of that reproach, the nature of Mary is excepted, the which is the nature that He took of her. For the flesh of Jesu Christ is the flesh of Mary, the which He bare above the stars in worshipping man above nature, and in worshipping more His mother.

Yet if He be son of the very mother, then it is a conceivable thing that she be mother of the same son. Not as to the unity of the person, but to the unity of bodily nature. If grace without property of especial and temporal nature may make unity, how much more then may the grace of corporal and especial nativity make unity of grace.

Like as the disciples in Jesu Christ of whom He saith Himself that, they be one, as we be. And after He saith :—'Father, I will that where I am they be with me.' And then if He will have with Him them that be joined so with Him in the faith, and that they be judges with Him, what shall then be judged of His mother? Where is she worthy to be but in the presence of her son? Therefore I understand and believe that the soul of Mary be honoured of her son by a right excellent prerogative, possessing her body glorified in Jesu Christ, whom she conceived. And why should not she possess her body glorified by which she conceived? For so great a hallowing is more worthy to be in Heaven than in earth.

The seat of God, the chamber of our Lord, and the worthy tabernacle of Jesu Christ, ought and appertaineth better to be there as He is, than elsewhere, and so right precious treasure is more worthy to be in Heaven than in earth.

And by right, no resolution of rottenness may follow so great entireness of thing not corruptible. And because I feel not that the right holy body be not delivered into meat of worms, I doubt to say it. And because that the gift of incomparable grace greatly surmounteth this estimation that I feel the consideration of many scriptures admonish me to say truth.

God saith sometime to His ministers:— 'Where I am there shall be My minister.' If this sentence be general to all them that have ministered Jesu Christ by faith and by work, how is there any more special than Mary? For without doubt

she was administress in all work.   For
she bare Him in her belly, she childed
Him, she nourished Him and laid Him
in the crib, she went with Him into Egypt,
and kept Him all her life unto the death
of the cross and departed not from Him,
but followed Him.

His divinity might not be incredible to
her, for she knew well that she had not
conceived of the seed of man but by
divine inspiration.   Then she having
faith in the power of her son, as of the
virtue of God not changeable, said,
when the wine failed :—'Son, they have
no wine.'   She wist that He might do
all things.   And He accomplished that
miracle.

Then seest thou that Mary was administress of Jesu Christ by faith and
work.   Then if she be not where Jesu
Christ will that his ministers be, where
shall she be then ?   And if she be there,
is it not by equal and like grace ?   And
if it be not equal, where is the equal
measure of God that rendereth to every
one after his desert ?   If by the desert
of Mary is given to living men much
grace, shall then the grace be lessened to
her being dead ?

Nay, nay, for if the death of all saints be precious, certainly, I judge the death of Mary to be right precious, which is received to the eternal joys by the justness of her son Jesu Christ, more honourably than the others, whom He had honoured by grace before His other saints.

And I say that she ought not to be put, and is not subject to the common humanity after death, that is to wit, of worms, of rottenness, and of powder, she that bare in her belly the Saviour of all men.

If the divine will vouchsafed to keep the vestments of the children from hurting among the flames of fire, why should not He then keep in His mother that which He kept in a strange vesture? It pleased Him to keep Jonas in the belly of the whale without corruption. Should not He then keep His mother not corrupt? He kept Daniel alive in the pit of lions from their distempered hunger. Ought He not to keep Mary for so many gifts of merits and dignities? And we know well that all these dignities that we have said have not kept nature, for we doubt not but grace hath kept more the entireness of Mary than nature.

And then our Lord maketh Mary to enjoy in her proper son, both in soul and in body, as she that never had touch nor spot of corruption in bringing forth so great a son. For she is always without corruption that was full of so much grace. She is living entirely, she that childed the Life of all.

And then, if I have said as I ought to say, Jesu Christ approve it, Thou and Thine; and if I have not said as I ought to say, I pray Thee to pardon me, Thou and Thine.

Printed by Roworth & Co. Ltd., Newton Street, W.C.

AN
OLD ENGLISH PARISH.

BY
J. CHARLES WALL.

Price 6s.

"A book of peculiar charm."—*Athenæum.*

It describes how the Church entered into the daily life, business, and pleasures of the people.

The donation, building, and consecration of the Church ; the furniture, vestments, and services in which the people took an active part. With illustrations from miniatures and other sources.

————

MEDIÆVAL WALL PAINTINGS.

BY
J. CHARLES WALL.

Price 2s. 6d.

The numerous paintings being uncovered by the removal of whitewash in English Churches, show how the walls were formerly a blaze of colour, depicting Bible scenes, Saints, etc. No other volume on this subject has been issued. The illustrations give a good idea of the paintings.

"It is most interesting, there is not a dull page between the covers."—*Guardian.*

————

TALBOT & CO.,
13, Paternoster Row, E.C.

THE
ANTIQUITIES OF GLASTONBURY.
BY
WILLIAM OF MALMESBURY.
Translated by F. LOMAX, B.A., B.C.L.

Price 2*s*.

An account of the very first Church founded
in Britain by Joseph of Arimathea.

THE MONASTIC CHURCH,
LASTINGHAM.

Price 1*s*.

The beautiful church, founded by St. Cedd,
on the Yorkshire Moors. The ancient Crypt
is a magnet which draws artists, scholars, and
antiquaries to the most charming country.

TALBOT & CO.,
13, Paternoster Row, E.C.

THEOS.

BY

M. KERCHEVER-ARNOLD.

Price 2s. 6d.

The Latin Vulgate and the Revised Version proved at fault in the noticeable reading from 1 *Tim.*, iii, 16.

The witness of the Alexandrian Codex freshly adduced from its photo-similes.

RECOGNITION AND LIFE IN THE BEYOND.

BY

M. KERCHEVER-ARNOLD.

Price 1s.   Post free, 1s. 1d.

TALBOT & CO.,
13, Paternoster Row, E.C.

CPSIA information can be obtained
at www.ICGtesting.com
Printed in the USA
BVHW041148301118
534441BV00007B/49/P